THE ST. LOUIS
ANTHOLOGY

MORE CITY ANTHOLOGIES BY BELT

THE ST. LOUIS ANTHOLOGY

Edited by Ryan Schuessler

Printed in the United States of America
First Edition 2019
ISBN: 978-1-948742-44-3

Belt Publishing
3143 W. 33rd Street, Cleveland, Ohio 44109
www.beltpublishing.com

Cover design by David Wilson
Interior design by Meredith Pangrace

contents

MEMORIES
The Moments That Shaped Us

contents

contents

EDITOR'S NOTE

St. Louis—the place so many of this book's contributors and readers call home—is on indigenous land. There was once a city of mounds here, that we now call Cahokia.

This land is the traditional, unceded homelands of the Illini Confederacy: the Cahokia, Kaskaskia, Michigamea, Moingwena, Peoria, and Tamaroa tribes; and also the Osage and Miami.

We also remember those who passed across this land during forced removals: the Cherokee, Delaware, Kickapoo, Sac and Fox, and Shawnee tribes, and others.

We thank them for their stewardship of this land, and offer our respect and gratitude to their elders, past and present.

INTRODUCTION

RYAN SCHUESSLER, WITH THE HELP OF
THE ST. LOUIS ANTHOLOGY'S CONTRIBUTORS

Most people picture the Arch as the recognizable symbol of St. Louis. Perhaps they should picture iron fences instead.

As Asher Kohn writes within this anthology: "St. Louis is built in brick, decorated in stone, and divided by seven-foot iron fences. These fences should be put in the outfield of Busch, sold in miniature at the Arch, and have children play on them at the City Museum. Their purpose is not to demarcate, but to remind passersby that they are not wholly welcome in the city their taxes pay for."

St. Louis is undoubtedly fragmented, physically so in that the city is dissected by rivers, highways, walls, and fences; but also in a more insidious way. It's a city (like many) where race, class, religion, and zip code might as well be cards in a rigged poker game, where the winners' prize is the ability to ignore that the losers have drastically shorter life expectancies.

But it's also a city of warmth, love, and beauty—especially in its contrasts. The people sipping rakija and dancing kolo in bars along Gravois are as St. Louis as those who grew up doing double Dutch outside Pruitt-Igoe. Midnight Annie and Stan Musial both built their legacies in this same city. The energy at the bottom of the ninth at Busch and the joy of a Juneteenth parade are both so St. Louis.

This anthology is a love letter to those moments—and all the others—that are so St. Louis. It's also an indictment of this fact: rare is the St. Louisan who can recognize them all. Rare is the St. Louisan who can see that the rage that burned down the QuikTrip on West Florissant after Mike Brown was killed, and the optimism of the little girls dancing in its parking the next morning, are both so St. Louis.

There are too many fences.

Within these pages I hope you find a cross section of the lives and stories that hold this city's crumbling bricks together. It will not be perfect. Despite all my intentions, I am limited by my own perspective. I am from St. Louis, and got dealt the lucky cards. There have been times during this project where I have undoubtedly fallen short.

What I am proud of, though, is that you will find many names you probably don't recognize, because a good number of this anthology's contributors are emerging writers, or aren't writers at all. These St. Louis stories have been written by St. Louisans themselves, not retold and curated through someone else's eyes and words.

From the beginning, my goal with this anthology was that it would transcend the fences Asher writes about, that it would expand beyond the voices one would expect in similar collections: the published writers, reporters, thinkers, and poets whose voices are amplified by our celebrated cultural and journalistic—mostly white—institutions, reinforcing a single narrative about the city and its people.

In this anthology, Galen Gritts reminds us that, for Native people living in St. Louis, the Arch is not just a recognizable symbol of civic pride. Vivian Gibson, Nick Sacco, and Steven Peebles paint a picture of what was lost in the name of urban development and progress. Ed Shimamoto, Miriam Morris, and Nartana Premachandra tell stories about the families that have lived, loved, hurt, and died outside of the idea that there is only "black St. Louis" and "white St. Louis." Sophia Benoit, Maja Sadikovic, and Lyndsey Ellis ask us to consider what "home" really means.

Like the Mississippi, St. Louis is many contradictory things all at once. It is slow moving, yet somehow constantly changing. It is a thing of commerce, a thing of entertainment, a beautiful thing. It can be placid or threatening. It is an avenue to other places and ideas. It can offer a seal of redemption, as a baptism does, or be the end, like the River Styx.

For every beautiful memory in St. Louis—collective or individual—there is grim reality lurking nearby. Yet in between the lines of every dark history sits resilience, unity, and humor. Too often, St. Louis seems to pick one or the other—nostalgia or trauma—erasing the people who have bravely faced both, living complex and nuanced lives in this city against a backdrop of its red brick, muddy rivers, and sticky summer nights when the symphony of cicadas and jazz is almost loud enough to drown out the gunshots.

In addition to the fences, rivers, and other things that fracture this city is that fine line—the one that divides St. Louis's nostalgia and its trauma.

This anthology dares to confront both.

blue thunder, red thunder

GALEN GRITTS

Gateway Arch reflects St. Louis' role in the Westward Expansion
News Headline

smiling, with the smoke clinging to the mountains over our heads
and the grass singing with growth under our feet, we smiled at your
coming and wondered at your companionship and became
baptists and methodists—joining hope to hope.

we were too small for the four corners to fight us, we were too
small like the squirrel and the otter. we were too small, we thought,
like you. but you came from beyond the air and earth and pitted
despair to death and forsook the ways of your fathers, exposing
the underside of the rock, exposing the shadow of the sun. but
somehow you buried the sun with that shadow, as no man would
have thought possible.

blue thunder, red thunder, but we were too small and our name
was not great nor is it now spoken, we have passed to gray
following the lost sun while you thrash wildly in your darkness.
yourself blue and red, power and death.
there is gnashing of teeth, but no wailing.

there's no one who knows us now, no one to miss our poverty
and hardship that you induced. we are made instead into
storybook heroes and noble antagonists,
the most villainous of circumstances.

you thought we have passed to gray,
following the lost sun.

you did not get us all.

HISTORIES

The People, Places, and Events that Define Us

Glimpses of History in an Old Stone Church

RON SCOTT

One of the loveliest park-like settings in St. Louis County, a retro island in the midst of suburban opulence, is not a park at all. Rather, the Old Meeting House, around which Geyer Road in Frontenac winds, is a nearly two-hundred year old church and cemetery. And, as might be expected of a structure and site that dates from the 1830s, it has stories to tell.

To fully appreciate the stories, of course, we need to understand the context. In 1830 the area that is now Frontenac was largely unsettled virgin land that had been part of the United States for fewer than three decades. Missouri, in fact, had been a state for only nine years. The "city" of St. Louis, an all-day ride away by horse or buggy, had fewer than 6,000 residents.

The earliest settlers were just arriving by 1830, pioneers from Kentucky and Tennessee (as well as Puritans and Baptists from New England), fleeing overcrowding, looking for fresh starts, or just seeking adventure. Most had little or nothing; even the most affluent from Appalachia brought only what possessions they could fit on small boats they could float down the Ohio and then laboriously push upstream to St. Louis. Some of these had a slave or two, and made them make the trip as well.

They settled on small tracts of land—typically eighty acres—purchased for only a few dollars from the government, built log cabins, and began farming with teams of horses or oxen. Where large houses with swimming pools now dot the landscape they dug wells or hauled water from streams; and where an upscale shopping mall now sits in Frontenac they butchered their own meat, grew their own vegetables and grain, and bartered for what they could not produce themselves. At best, theirs was a hardscrabble existence.

They also brought their religion with them, the Calvinism of Appalachia; so, not surprisingly, small Presbyterian churches began to spring up. One of the earliest was called Des Peres, after a village located on the nearby Des Peres River. Organized in 1832, the small group of families met for worship in a private home. The families included names like Geyer, McCutcheon, and Maddox—now familiar street names.

In 1833 three families donated an acre of land each, and a stone one-room building was built on the Geyer-Maddox Road, a wagon trail that went south to the Manchester Road (which connected St. Louis to the new capitol in Jefferson City). The wagon trail separated the church building from the cemetery. Early preachers, many of whom rode to the church from St. Louis, included a missionary from New England named Elijah Parish Lovejoy, who had walked to St. Louis from Maine in 1827.

Lovejoy was a passionate abolitionist who began the *St. Louis Observer*, a fiery tract that mixed religion, politics, and local happenings with strong opinions. Run out of Missouri by pro-slavery elements, Lovejoy moved across the Mississippi to Alton, hoping for a more accepting climate in the "free" state of Illinois. But opponents followed him, and ultimately murdered him in 1837—the first American martyr to a free press.

So conflicting themes of the young nation intersected in a small church in rural St. Louis County: Appalachian Calvinists and New England Puritans; southern slave owners and northern abolitionists; all seeking new opportunities, new lives. This was pre-Civil War America, boiled down to its elements, in the idyllic setting of the frontier. What must it have been like in the little stone building on Geyer-Maddox Road?

Well, there are clues. Lovejoy did not preach for an extended period at Des Peres. There is reason to believe slaves were buried in the southeast corner of the church's graveyard. In 1837 the congregation, led by its pastor Gary Hickman, voted to align with the "old school" (southern) tradition as the Presbyterian Church in America split along economic and political (slavery) lines. Between 1837 and 1874, records show that the Des Peres Church received 161 new members; in 1874, the church had forty-four members on the rolls.

Those were turbulent times. But turbulent times come and go, and life proceeds apace. Churches (or schools, or other institutions) are not immune from the impact of society. But people and their institutions change: today, the little stone church is part of Faith Des Peres Presbyterian, one of the most liberal Presbyterian churches in the area.

There is good and evil in everything, including all of us. Slavery was evil; but were the people of the early Des Peres Church evil? They were children of their time, products of their culture, limited by what they knew about life. It has always been so, and it always will be so.

Segregation in Heaven

MARK LOEHRER

On a sunny Saturday afternoon in 1907, Bertha Williams opened her front door to find a curious sight.

A group of well-dressed white businessmen, led by Father McDonald of St. Ann Parish in the Vandeventer neighborhood, had come to see her. Their business? To petition Bertha to leave the neighborhood. It was the group's third stop. They were a collection of residents in the middle-class, largely white neighborhood. Their day's goal was to politely request their black neighbors to move out. So far, they had enjoyed little success.

The group's first stop in the neighborhood was at the home of L. T. Traddock, a renter who worked as a clerk with the postal service. When confronted by the group and asked to consider the idea of living elsewhere, Traddock replied, "I have never liked this house, ever since I moved here a few months ago. But since my neighbors are so anxious to be rid of me, I shan't overwork myself from now on in seeking a new place of residence." Perhaps facing such a terse rebuke of their petitions, the group had thought Bertha would be more receptive; she was after all, a schoolteacher.

Bertha Williams graduated from Sumner High School and Normal, an institution that thrived during the era of school segregation, employing black PhDs in science and literature to educate generations of black high school students in St. Louis, because black PhDs could often find no other employer. According to Warice Blackmon-Davis, president of the Sumner Alumni Association, Sumner's record of academic excellence was proof that even within the imperfection of segregation, perfection was still achievable.

Answering her door, Bertha found herself eye to eye with Father Owen Justus McDonald. McDonald was an Irish immigrant who had built his parish, located at Page and Whittier, into an impressive institution on the city's west side. McDonald was well-known throughout the diocese as being the first to found a free, parochial school—attached to St. Ann Parish. He was also an active and outspoken leader in the Welfare Association, the organization that would sponsor and campaign on behalf of the 1916 Segregation Ordinance in St. Louis. McDonald begged Williams to accept the group's petition to leave the neighborhood. He argued, from a theological perspective, that segregation of the races was a moral and Christian concept. Bertha replied pointedly, "Will segregation be practiced in heaven, father?"

After the priest lost all hope that the schoolteacher would accept the invitation to leave out of faith in religion, the group next hoped to convince Bertha Williams to vacate by offering monetary compensation. After refusing their offers, Bertha remarked, "I am open to the proposition to sell the property. I paid $4000 for it. But if the control of it is so valuable to my neighbors, I will sell it at a substantial increase on my purchase price."

The group left Bertha Williams's residence without making a successful offer. This jarring incident provides one of the earliest twentieth-century examples of an attitude towards residential segregation in St. Louis, but it would not be the last.

"Segregation in Heaven" was first published in the St. Louis Post-Dispatch on July, 13, 1907.

Decoding the Veiled Prophet

DEVIN O'SHEA

A rogue debutante in the Kiel Center balcony took a loose cable in hand, swooped down to the stage far below, fractured her rib upon impact, and was still able to run up to the Veiled Prophet of Khorassan and pull the hood off. In 1972, this revealed white-guy executive, Tom K. Smith—the vice president of Monsanto—seated on the throne.

The rogue debutante was Gena Scott, a member of a protest group called ACTION, which was led by one St. Louis's most iconic civil rights leaders, Percy Green. *The St. Louis Post-Dispatch* never published Tom Smith's unveiled face. However, this incident and the many ACTION protests shamed and publicized the Veiled Prophet (VP) enough that the tradition retreated from St. Louis public life. It continues today in private.

Once a year, the Veiled Prophet emerges for the VP Ball. Pictures of the debutantes grace *Ladue News*, and the glossy cover of *Town & Style*. The VP is protected by a layer of confusing folk history that's manufactured by the city's wealthiest families, and our collective indifference. St. Louis never fully grappled with what the VP organization is, where it came from, and what we might still do about it.

In contrast to the recently toppled Confederate monument, which stood on Forest Park's north side from 1914 to 2016, the VP is more secretive and harder to decipher as a racist symbol.

While there are a few different versions of the VP, he's normally depicted wearing white gloves, robes, and he sometimes carries a wizard's staff. According to a 1950s VP Ball storybook, his preferred mode of transport was a magic carpet. In an 1883 poster, he's depicted atop a mythical griffin because, as we all know, he has to fly to St. Louis from Khorassan—a dreamland somewhere in the Orient. At the time of the VP's conception, this was a common practice. The white European/American imagination knew nothing of a place called "the Middle East" except that it existed on a map. Even educated scholars in 1880s America had little access to what anything east of Turkey was actually like. Like Oz or Middle Earth, the Orient was a fantasyland; perfect for the Western imagination to run wild inside—often resulting in homespun, incredibly harmful, racial stereotyping that's still with us today. What's notable is that the VP was a despot in this faraway place.

Sometimes the VP has a long Santa Claus beard, but his face is supposed to be shrouded beneath a long, lace veil. In some of these depictions, the VP's face resembles a standard old white man; think Father Time or the biblical Abraham. However, in the first depiction, he resembled a rifle-wielding Mardi Gras clown.

The very first image of the VP was an 1877 woodcut. He wields two muskets and a pistol, and he's ready for violence. Instead of a veil, he has large, black, triangular eyes which look as though they were cut from the same black felt that composes his eyebrows and triangular nose. The steeple of his carnivalesque hat is decorated with two wizard's stars. He wears a bandit's white kerchief around his neck, and the expression on his face can only be described as dreadful; something between agony and intimidation.

These symbols are not haphazard: the VP debuted in the *Missouri Republican* to crush the Great Railroad Strike of 1877.

In 1877, St. Louis participated in the country's first-ever general strike. The railroad men of the Workingman's Party had the dangerous job of running the city's system of transportation. A network of streetcars, the romanticized riverboats, and trains, trains, trains were the lifeblood of the city. The strike shut it all down. Thus, the city fathers were in a bind.

The woodcut appeared with this threat which doesn't exactly roll off the tongue: "It will be readily observed from the accoutrements of the Prophet that the procession is not likely to be stopped by street cars or anything else." In other words, the Veiled Prophet will shoot his way through any picket line he encounters.

The mayor of this time had an exceptionally long name: Mayor Henry Clemens von Overstolz. He, the city's blue bloods, and the business leaders were electrically terrified by both the 1871 Paris Commune—a socialist revolt in France—and the St. Louis strike's inclusion of black workers. This was a rare example of solidarity between black and white St. Louis workers. The leaders of the strike formed an Executive Committee (EC) which was headed up by leftists and union organizers like James McCarthy, the attorney who communicated with the mayor on the committee's behalf. What we know about EC: they didn't get along. Leaders disagreed on how to conduct negotiation. They wanted improved wages, a ban on child labor, and an eight-hour work day, and the EC locked itself away in its own negotiations for so long that the blue-blooded gentry, and Mayor von Overstolz, were able to organize.

Formerly Confederate artillery was put on display beside the gallows near City Hall and on Thursday, the police, national guard, and an *ad hoc* militia massed in Lafayette Park. They marched north and broke the strike at its headquarters in Schuller's Hall, a building which stood in Old North St. Louis and was eventually sacrificed for the Mark Twain Expressway (Highway 44).

It's unclear what the strikers made of the VP woodcut, but the guy never showed up. Instead, unarmed strikers faced police cavalry, bayonets, and cannons. The VP made his first physical appearance the next year during the VP parade.

It's important to understand that shows of force in the streets, and parades of this time, are a theatrical ancestor of WWE *SmackDown*. In a pre-film world, the parade was a cultural explosion.

While the educational merits of *SmackDown* are debatable, late-nineteenth-century spectacles were also meant to "instruct" the underclasses. Immigrants, factory workers, idlers, and the farmers took in a spectacular amount of propaganda this way. And instead of turning off the TV, these demonstrations of power came right through the working-class neighborhoods.

In 1878, a year after the strike, the first VP parade followed the first VP Debutante Ball. Atop a float in white, the VP rode through downtown St. Louis, around the Chamber of Commerce, and down Broadway near the Old Court House. Standing beside the VP was a bloody executioner in a black hood. This first VP's identity (with the rhyming title and name) ran in the newspapers: Chief of Police John Priest.

Brief accounts of the VP's origin stop with the strike. The origin story is usually not explained. Why would a Veiled Prophet of Khorassan choose to visit St. Louis?

According to a 1952 VP Ball pamphlet, things were going so well in Khorassan that the VP wanted to bestow the fruits of his despotic rule upon a deserving people. In Goldilocks fashion, he rode his magic carpet over Egypt and decided the Egyptians wouldn't listen. Next, he discovered all of Europe was "too set in its ways." Finally, for some reason, St. Louis, Missouri, fit just right.

While Khorassan Province is a real part of modern-day Iran, the VP of Khorassan has 100 percent nothing to do with it. This legend is courtesy of the Irish poet, Thomas Moore. Tommy Moore—the famously short, wildly popular nineteenth-century writer—went through a phase of imagining orientalist parable poems. Moore's VP is the first of *Lalla Rookh*'s four parables. Tommy called his character the VP based off Al-Muqanna, a real-life Persian ruler circa 779 AD, who may have also been a chemist—a hobby which ended in a horrifically disfiguring explosion. To save everyone the pain of looking at his ugly mug, he wore a veil.

Moore took that legend and warped the VP into a despotic ruler who, like Moses, caught a gnostic glimpse of Allah. Therefore, Moore's VP claimed he had a deific face. This VP is the corrupter of the word of God. He rallies his people to a greedy war of conquest, and when things go wrong, the cowardly VP commands his followers to commit suicide. He follows suit after vowing to return in a divine resurrection-y way.

This parable is supposed to be about blindly loyal followers, despotic rulers, and insane cycles of violence. But some St. Louisan in 1877 read about the hubris of this cultish leader and said, "Cool. Really cool. What an awesome story." That person was the ex-Confederate cavalry officer extraordinaire, Alonzo Slayback.

Not only a wealthy businessman/lawyer, Alonzo Slayback was also the founding father of the VP Society. As a (bad) poet himself, Slayback likely read *Lalla Rookh* along with everyone else at the time. Slayback's poems were largely about the noble lost cause of the Confederacy. Many explained that his time as cavalry officer for General Lee meant he was a winner, and very cool. He loved himself a secret rich-boy club and modeled the VP on New Orleans's Mystic Krewe of Comus. Slayback was also shot dead by the editor of the *Post-Dispatch*—killed during an argument. Neat guy.

For Slayback, it didn't matter that *Lalla Rookh*'s VP was a villain. It provided a literary context—however dubious—for the secret club they formed after the strike. Why you need scholarly cover for your club leads to the least-understood aspect of the Veiled Prophet: his vigilantism.

The strike-breaking VP looked like a Klansman; Thomas Moore's VP did not.

In May 1866, eleven years before the strike, the Ku Klux Klan was founded by former Confederate soldiers in Pulaski, Tennessee. In costume, the Ku Klux Klan was above the police. The trend of ex-Confederates donning a hood to break the law and harass the citizenry—especially newly freed slaves—spread in the early 1870s as a way to rebel against Reconstruction.

The first wave of the KKK was an outbreak of domestic terrorism that gets overshadowed by the second wave in the 1920s. It's important to note that the second wave standardized their symbols and uniform: white pointed-steeple hat with two eye slits, white robes, and a burning cross. That's the KKK we know. That's what stuck in our collective memory as *the* symbol of white supremacy and racism. The first-wave Klansmen didn't look like that.

In the first wave, Klansmen dressed in homemade costume. They were puckish, cheap, local theatre characters. Many had felt, or cotton, wizard's beards and this initial Klan dress harkened back to a European folklore tradition called *charivari*. As Elaine Parsons writes in *Ku-Klux: The Birth of the Klan During Reconstruction*, *charivari* was a kind of vigilante shaming ritual that enforced the village law about "sexual immorality, gambling, drinking, or socializing across racial lines; of theft, fraudulent trading, or fencing stolen goods; or of holding unpopular views." After the Civil War, this costuming was adopted by the Ku Klux Klan to reassert white supremacy as the dominant law of post-war America, a tradition which continues today.

Around 1871, Congress passed the Enforcement Act, which prosecuted Klan activities. Six years later, in the 1877 Railroad Strike, most would have recognized the VP as a first-wave Klansman.

The second wave obscured the Veiled Prophet's symbols; he doesn't have a white pointy hat or a burning cross. The early connection between the VP and the KKK is never admitted by the VP Society, but the evidence, to recap, is all there. The first wave of Klansmen were ex-Confederates like Alonzo Slayback. As an amature poet, Slayback would have read *Lalla Rookh* and noticed that Thomas Moore's Veiled Prophet conveniently covers his head with a hood. Or, as a member of the Mystic Krewe of Comus (which has deep Confederate ties), Slayback witnessed a parade with the poem as its theme in New Orleans. When it came time to break the 1877 strike, the first wave of the KKK had been in the newspapers since the 1860s.

Klansman or not, the VP expressed a Klan-ish willingness to commit violence outside the law and re-establish the social order.

There are overlapping aspects of the VP which have little consistency beyond this: the VP is a character of oppression whose story has been rewritten over and over. The figure is a *charivari* Klansman, an orientalist despot from Thomas Moore's imagination, and a carnivalesque knight shipped up the Mississippi River from the middle of a New Orleans Mardi Gras parade. The VP is all of these with no true center.

At the end, this character was, and remains, a tool to illustrate the superiority of the St. Louis elite. Since 1878, the city fathers who comprised the VP Society shaped St. Louis in their favor. Their names are chiseled on buildings; they are familiar characters in the local imagination: Meritz, Schnuck, Busch, Taylor, Schlafly, Desloge, McCarthy, Danforth.

The modern VP debutantes *do* perform admirable volunteer work. According to veiledprophet.org, there is a robust "philanthropic arm of the VP organization," but that is no excuse for continuing a Confederate tradition. It is absolutely shameful that in 2018, the St. Louis mayor participated in the VP parade on the Fourth of July. Alonzo Slayback's vision for the city is still alive and well.

So what do we do? Do we need another Gena Scott? Do we need another ACTION council and another Percy Green? Yes, absolutely. But what happens if the VP is unveiled again? Should the city expunge this character from its history? Or is this story still malleable? The supposed power of this figure might still be rewritten. If he hasn't already, the despotic VP could be turned into the St. Louis fool, the dolt with a tablecloth on his head who attempted to stand in the way of community, equality, and solidarity.

Song of the Mississippi

JANE ELLEN IBUR

for Hosea Jackson

If I could be like water I would flow
with tugs, boats, and barges riding my back,
flanked on either bank by paths and trails,
all along the shore piles of driftwood.
My clothes and me all made of water
hurry to rendezvous with the sea.

I'm a confined being, a river not the sea.
All I concentrate on is the constant flow
praying I never run out of water.
In droughts I pray for a comeback
my bones dry and white as driftwood
which clog both the flow of water and the hiking trails

leaving some animals dying, birds picking at entrails,
hoping their spirits will mingle with the sea,
genesis of all life. My spirit rides a driftwood
ferry, aiming for the other shore to syncopate with the flow
of the river, proud and straight as my back.
On the shore an empty greenhouse contemplates rebirth, water

her necessity. So close she sits to vast water
unreachable. Buckets ferried down trails
help to bring old life back
with respect and honor, treated with decency.
Echoes of good advice, go with the flow,
ride the current like a piece of driftwood.

I eat trees, spitting chunks of driftwood
like seeds that float like rafts on water.
I match my breathing with the flow
floating as the currents create eddies and water trails
whose sole determination is to reach the sea
where everything changes, no going back

fighting a fierce current. The past waits back
there like coals in a pile of dry driftwood
ready to spark. Steady as the sea
I smother the memories deep in water
shut down all the access trails.
Thirty trees line the bank hoping for a taste of overflow.

No turning back, no existing without water
or we turn dead as driftwood blocking the trails.
I imitate the sea, continue to flow.

Where Wild Plums Bloom

ALICE AZURE

for Charlene Walking Bull

It must have been his larger-than-life
confidence, tall, handsome looks—maybe
his nickname "Bull" or resemblance
to the father she hardly knew—that drew her
to him. Maybe she was glad to find a man
with a steady job at the Anheuser-Busch brewery,
able to buy a house in East St. Louis
with a plum tree orchard, extra lots for his garden,
room for his trucks, his vintage cars, his motorcycle—
good times for all his friends—
but never a wedding band for her.

Only five when her mother died, her father
put her and two sisters in a children's home.
Some called this *spiritual protection* for the little girl
strangely blessed by spirit visitations, and penny-colored
hair like her famous ancestor Crazy Horse.

In the early sixties, she wanted to become a lawyer.
Not practical for an Indian girl said her counselors.
Turning her back, she left the Whitehall Children's Home
and the hovering shadows of Oglala kin.

Nothing stopped the advancing wasteland
from their East St. Louis home—
boarded-up businesses, houses gone vacant,
empty lots littered with chunks
of jagged foundations,
unchecked Hustler Clubs,
food pantries, pawn places,
young people crowded on sagging front porches,
sitting in the sun on picnic benches, waiting
for jobs, better times, for their fixes.

Still, she strung Christmas lights and a wooden "Jesus" sign
on the chain-link fence around their home,
took good care of him, their daughters, son, all the other
children and grandchildren.
Now Bull is gone, passed on—her kinship vows released.
Wild plum blossoms sprout their thousand, fragile flowers
over East St. Louis and on the Pine Ridge Reservation.

Oh, spirits of her Oglala kin!
Bring to fruition the gifts you have given.
Grant her confidence in her vision.

Lombards and Sicilians:
The Forgotten History of Italian Immigration to St. Louis

NICK SACCO

A couple with a young baby and a single bag of belongings optimistically look into the distance toward a new American frontier. The man's stylish suit and finely trimmed mustache belie a rugged demeanor, while the woman's embrace of her child and quiet confidence exude personal strength. Their lives have been shaped by years of struggle in the Old World, but they have worked tirelessly for a better future for their child. This is the moment in which they can finally call themselves Americans. Both have their left foot moving forward, ready to tackle any challenges that may come their way in the land of the free.

Sculpted by St. Louis native Rudolph Torrini in 1972, and located next to Saint Ambrose Catholic Church, "The Italian Immigrants" dramatically portrays Italian migration to the Hill at the turn of the twentieth century. For those of us with Italian ancestry living in St. Louis, the symbolic (and appetizing) center of our cultural identity is the Hill, a vibrant Italian American enclave located in the southwestern corner of the city's limits. Within the Hill's boundaries sits this statue that tells an important story about immigration to this area.

For me, "The Italian Immigrants" statue was once a tangible symbol of Italian American unity. I understood from a young age that many American-born white residents at that time looked upon my ancestors with skepticism and disdain. Nevertheless I could take pride in knowing that Italians tried to support their families and build a successful community far away from the confines of the Old World. The Italian immigrants of St. Louis worked hard, supported their new homeland during both World Wars, and in some cases enjoyed real financial prosperity. While the Hill remains an important gathering place for dinner, bocce ball, and family outings, the "The Italian Immigrants" statue establishes a sense of history and memory within St. Louis's Italian Americans. It builds continuity with the past and instills pride for our ancestors.

But what if these stories of Italian unity and a smooth transition towards American belonging are more complex than anything portrayed on a sculpture? What if the Hill's existing landscape masks as much as it reveals about Italian immigration to St. Louis? My understanding of this history—my family's history—was challenged when I came across a newspaper feature on the Hill from 1901 that offers subtle clues into a legacy of exclusion, racism, and class conflict among St. Louis Italians.

The earliest settlement of Italian immigrants to the Hill began around 1882. While popular lore dramatizes the trip from Europe to New York City's Ellis Island (which was not built until 1892), a good number of Italian immigrants to St. Louis actually came by way of New Orleans. Traveling up the Mississippi River, many Italians arriving in the city came to work in the clay mines, brickyards, and factories of Cheltenham, an area just south of present-day Forest Park. Here the business of extracting clay and manufacturing bricks thrived. Some laborers did not intend to stay in the United States permanently and chose to work a few years, save their money, and go back home. But the Italians as a group soon developed a reputation as hard workers. Many of the 900 Italians who decided to stay in St. Louis in the 1880s settled just south of the mines at "St. Louis Hill," the highest point in the city. By 1900 the city's Italian population had grown by more than 60 percent and those living near Cheltenham took to calling their community "Dago Hill." Homes, schools, grocery stores, bakeries, and eventually Saint Ambrose Church emerged to provide stability, education, jobs, and religious instruction to its residents.

The *St. Louis Post-Dispatch* reporter who came to visit Dago Hill in May 1901 sought to educate other St. Louis residents about this growing Italian community. He noted that the trip from Italy to St. Louis cost fifty dollars and that most laborers at the clay mines and brickyards made between $1.35 and $1.50 a day. Not only were wages far better than anything that could be earned in Italy, but the chance to acquire land and property was much higher. Amid a weak economy and huge landholdings owned by a small wealthy elite, young Italians in the last quarter of the nineteenth century looked to the United States for a better future.

In the course of interviewing residents of Dago Hill, the reporter noted the comments of one anonymous, yet vocal resident. The resident proudly boasted that while there were "plenty of them little black fellows here [in St. Louis]," they were thankfully excluded from Dago Hill. "They all downtown," he proclaimed. He was not talking about African Americans, however. He was talking about Sicilians.

"The Italians of the hill are particular that they be recognized as people from the north of Italy," the reporter noted. "They put the north on their clubhouse, their community store, the store delivery wagons, their flags and upon their society stationary. They want the world to know that they do not come from South Italy or the Island of Sicily. They say they are a lighter of complexion, larger of frame and further advanced in intelligence than their fellow-countrymen of the south." In describing his community to the reporter, the proud resident also mentioned that St. Louis Sicilians were lazy and socially undesirable outcasts. "They push the banana carts. North Italian works," he boasted.

It turns out that the Hill was not a place of Italian American unity but instead a community for northern Italians who first and foremost viewed themselves as Lombards. In his book *Immigrants on the Hill*, historian Gary Mormino points out that many of the Hill's residents came primarily from the small town of Cuggiono, Lombardy, not far from the border with Switzerland. The proud resident in 1901 had explicitly stated what was well known on the Hill: in the course of settling in St. Louis, Italian Lombards had created their own racial hierarchy. In a demonstration of the fluid and subjective nature of racial distinctions, they proclaimed themselves as white and Sicilians as black.

These racial distinctions were no doubt influenced by American racial attitudes. White Americans treated all Italian immigrants with hostility, but as the Hill's Lombards gradually worked to establish their whiteness, they benefited in their own way from St. Louis's institutional racism. To cite but one example, many Lombards were able to secure bank loans to purchase their own homes. For Sicilians outside the Hill, such a possibility rarely existed. My Sicilian-born great-great grandfather, Julio Sacco, immigrated to St. Louis around 1890 and worked as a shoemaker downtown for almost fifty years. Unable to read, write, or speak English, Julio drifted from one shanty tenement to another, and from job to job, while searching for financial security. The results of this lifetime of toil were less than ideal. When he died of a heart attack in 1938 at age sixty-eight, Julio had never owned a home and possessed little money to his name.

When I see "The Italian Immigrants" sculpture on the Hill today, I think of the many "black" Sicilians like my great-great grandfather who were once excluded from the Hill. In retrospect, this statue was never meant to be theirs to claim. Instead, the statue is a commemoration of "The *Northern* Italian Immigrants." The heroic couple symbolize Lombard heritage: light skinned, well-dressed, "civilized," and *the right kind of immigrant* to America. The historical record of the Hill—census records, newspaper articles, family heirlooms, and memories—portrays a complex reality that shadows the statue's mythical, soft glow.

The Sicilians who immigrated to St. Louis settled in "Little Italy," an area in north St. Louis that has been long forgotten by most locals today. Roughly bordered by Sixth and Ninth Streets (east to west) and O'Fallon and Morgan Streets (north to south), the community encompassed roughly fifteen city blocks. The Sicilians who arrived in the 1880s and 1890s were mostly poor laborers working in manual labor, shoemaking, and at the V. Viviano Macaroni Manufacturing Company. Some women worked jobs as well, especially in the garment industry.

Little Italy had its own successful food culture. According to historian Eleanore Berra Marfisi, there were thirty-five fresh fruit merchants in Little Italy in 1918, and by the 1950s a thriving market called "Produce Row" provided jobs and a sense of community to the area's residents. Like many others, the Sacco family experienced its closest, most intimate moments at the dinner table. While the family doesn't possess any written recipes from the time, we know that great-great grandmother Rose would have shopped on Produce Row and cooked many traditional Italian favorites, particularly homemade bread, pasta, and red meat sauce.

Most of these residents would have worshipped at several Catholic churches in the area. Saint Patrick's (originally built in 1843 for the city's Irish Catholics and located at Sixth and Biddle) and Our Lady Help of Christians (established in 1900 and located at Tenth and Cole) were the most popular. A third church at Twenty-third and Mullanphy, Saint Leo, was primarily Irish but also welcomed Sicilians, including the Sacco family. When Julio died, the family held the funeral at Saint Leo. And for many years an annual "Hill Festa Day" took place in Little Italy until 1973 that brought together residents' shared love of food, Sicily, and God in a day of exciting festivities.

Significant changes after World War II doomed Little Italy to a slow extinction. City planners developed blueprints for Interstate Highway 70, a convention center, and the construction of tenement housing designed primarily for low-income African American residents. Saint Patrick's, Our Lady Help of Christians, and Saint Leo were closed and demolished in the 1970s. The Cervantes Convention Center was completed in 1977, and by 1995 the area was expanded to include both the America's Center Convention Complex and the Trans World Airlines Dome (now Edward Jones Dome), home of the now-departed St. Louis Rams football team.

Sensing this changing racial dynamic and the threat of eminent domain abuse, the area's Sicilians began moving to the Hill—where interethnic conflict softened during and after World War II—and to the suburbs of St. Louis County. The shared fight against European fascism undoubtedly helped St. Louis Italians find a common purpose among themselves. As St. Louis Sicilians came to the Hill, they enjoyed the benefits of bank loans, home ownership, and escape from urban decay. They began their own transition to whiteness as a singular Italian American identity gradually formed around the Hill. "Lombards" and "Sicilians" were no more.

Few St. Louisans would have felt sorrow about the loss of Little Italy when the Rams won the Super Bowl in 2000. The displacement of longtime residents from the area and heavy investment in urban renewal appeared to be worth the cost at the time. But today when I see the empty, overgrown parking lot where Saint Patrick's was once located, I can't help but feel a sense of personal loss; a loss not just for any particular family, but a city struggling to promote growth and renewal. Many Italian American families who once lived in St. Louis, mine included, played a leading role in the mass postwar white flight away from the city. They began moving to places like North County—Ferguson, Florissant, and Hazelwood—and, starting in the 1990s, continued the move to St. Charles County.

The affection many feel towards the Hill is nonexistent towards Little Italy since its cultural history has been erased from the built landscape. My family had little understanding of this history until recently. Indeed, my mother was shocked to hear that the Sacco family's American roots started in Little Italy and not the Hill. "I didn't even know Little Italy existed," she once admitted.

But as Gary Mormino points out, "Once there were many Little Italies and Dago Hills; alas, they have grown fewer."

Merluzzo

SOPHIA BENOIT

My father has been trying—mostly with terrible results—to entice me to come back to St. Louis for seven years. Well, the first year after I left for school in the "lost, anchorless, soulless" city of Los Angeles (his words), he didn't have to do much. I had a boyfriend back in St. Louis and was coming back often anyway. After that ended, however, the price of flights somehow felt every penny of their $350. First it was staying in LA for its mild summers, where not a single person decries that it's "not the heat, it's the humidity." Eventually, I worked my way up to missing Thanksgiving, something that has left me wracked with guilt (although most things do, so it's not a great barometer).

Once my father caught on to the fact that my trips were going to become less and less frequent—though still about three times a year, which is pretty great if I do say so myself—and that my life in Los Angeles was becoming permanent, he had to get more creative with the enticements. First, it was mostly shooting related: "We can do target practice in the garage if Katy isn't home" (This piece may be how my stepmother finds out about that). "Do your friends in California have guns?" (They do not).

Anything that seemed antithetical to the Missourian image of what California stands for was fodder for him. We're having pork steaks; come home. We got illegal fireworks; you should come home. There's a family of foxes living under the porch and I'm feeding them rotisserie chickens from Schnucks; come back before they leave. Once, I came home to find him building a makeshift trampoline under our front porch light because a nest of baby birds was going to learn to fly soon and he had really taken to them. God knows how the other baby birds of the world make it without the careful attention of my father.

Eventually, he changed tactics: food. It's a smart move, since he's a great cook and I'm an even better eater. This isn't typical St. Louis food, however. He doesn't try to get me to come home with promises of concretes or toasted ravioli. There isn't Provel cheese on the table.

Sometimes it's something as simple as him wanting to try out the pressure cooker, which never really seems to work properly; the risk of explosion is half the fun. Recently, he wanted to try out a new sausage shop. It's easy to lure me back in winter months, since every New Year we make bagna cauda, a dish of melted butter, oil, garlic, salt, and anchovies that you then dip vegetables and bread into. Despite the name, which means "hot bath" in Italian, the dish itself is a revelation, as most things made of melted butter are. We also often make jars of homemade pesto to give out as Christmas gifts.

Don't steal this idea, but homemade pesto is an amazing gift. Store-bought pesto will quickly disappoint after you've made it fresh. I know that sounds like something Ina Garten would say, but it's the truth. When I was younger, each of us five kids had a specific job when it came to making pesto, whether it was grating cheese, chopping nuts, or mine, which was to carefully cut the basil plant leaves. Recently, I was home for one of my father's quarterly trips to Viviano's. I'm not even sure that they sell anything he couldn't find elsewhere, but I think being in a shop full of Italian food makes him feel at home. As usual, my father got salted cod. It took twenty-five years of trying to wear me down before this time, mostly out of guilt that I'm not home enough, I agreed to "try" it. I don't particularly like fish, but he told me the story of his Nonna making *merluzzo*, the Italian word for cod, but also the general name they used for a dish of cod, onions, and polenta. Polenta was really the selling point for me. There's almost nothing you can make out of corn meal I won't eat.

My grandfather came from a town outside of Turin called Salto, which means "to leap." An appropriately named place to leave, I suppose. Upon visiting the town, however, any modern American would wonder at leaving; it's overwhelmingly beautiful. Nestled in the verdant foothills of (the also appropriately named) Piedmont, my family that is still there lives on a small, mostly defunct vineyard from the early 1800s, surrounded by a not-at-all-defunct fruit orchard. They're a family of butchers, a job that seems to be from another time, and which only adds to the charm of visiting.

When my grandfather left, however, the area was struggling; his father left first and stayed in America for seven years, going through Ellis Island before arriving in the Italian enclave of Collinsville, Illinois. There he established a blacksmith shop and eventually sent for his wife and two sons. When my grandfather arrived, the story goes, he was placed in school a few years lower than his actual age, mostly because he didn't speak any English. This strategy seems a bit odd to me: why would fourth-grade English be any easier than sixth-grade English? Perhaps out of the frustration at this process, he vowed that once he learned English, he would not speak Italian again. This is how my family lost the language, a source of an odd amount of grief for some of us. When you tell someone that your father is Italian or that your grandfather is, one of the first questions is "So, do you speak Italian?" Plus, there's nothing more magical to monolingual Americans than little babies and children who can seamlessly slip between two languages. We were robbed of that, but the food stayed.

For as much as my grandfather tried to divorce himself from the language, he still competed in Bocce tournaments and became a butcher, just like his family back home. And his children all learned to grow basil for homemade pesto, and "flip" the pot of polenta, letting it spill onto the counter to harden, and melt anchovies for banga cauda.

That's because you don't lose your home when you leave; you carry small, surprising pieces of it with you. When I came to Los Angeles—admittedly a much shorter cultural jump than moving from Italy—I brought some of St. Louis. I still wave "thank you" at other drivers if they let me in. I refuse to call anything a "freeway." I feed people every time they come to my house. I have mastered a gooey butter cake recipe. I was the only person in my friend group who knew that the animal we encountered in the bushes on campus was just a possum. I prefer thin crust pizza, although I'm not sure you can say that's a St. Louis thing. I'm still better than average at cornhole. I love a good trip to Target. In many ways, I am distinctly midwestern.

Someday, I might have to get my own children to come back to me. I won't use cod. I'll probably stick with gooey butter cake.

A Gift to St. Louis

ED SHIMAMOTO, DAVE SHIMAMOTO, DICK SHIMAMOTO

On December 7, 1941, as young George Shimamoto walked home from his strawberry fields in Lodi, California, a neighbor rushed toward him.

"The Japanese just bombed Pearl Harbor!" the neighbor, an old Scot, shouted.

Shimamoto, then twenty-eight, grinned. He thought the man was kidding.

"No, really. It's on the radio," his neighbor replied.

"You're joking," Shimamoto answered.

"What do you think they'll do to you?"

"Me? Why would they do anything to me? I haven't done anything wrong." Shimamoto was stunned by the question as much as he was by the news of the attack.

That night George and Kimi Shimamoto, with their one-month-old son, listened with millions of others to the radio news. Like other Americans they were shocked and angry. And their neighbor's question haunted them.

This is an account of what happened nearly eighty years ago, but it rings clearly each September, when we—George and Kimi's three sons—participate with dozens of volunteers in putting together the annual Japanese Festival at the Missouri Botanical Garden in St. Louis, one of the city's most popular Labor Day weekend attractions. Amidst the chaos leading up to the festival, there are brief moments of calm to reflect on our family's journey since that fateful day in December 1941.

The answer to our father's question came in February 1942 when President Roosevelt ordered the evacuation and relocation of some 110,000 Japanese Americans, most of whom lived along the Pacific Coast. While a few evacuees were able to sell their property, albeit at a terrible loss, most, like our parents, were forced by the War Relocation Authority to abandon everything they owned, except what each could carry.

"At first, they put us in horse stalls on the San Joaquin County Fairground in Stockton, California. We lived there and slept on hay stuffed mattresses for six months while they built barracks," our father recalled to a reporter years later.

In the fall of 1942, our family was among 9,000 internees who entered the gates of the Rohwer Relocation Center near McGehee, Arkansas, one of ten internment camps in the interior United States. Our parents, with young Dick, lived in just one room, furnished with a mattress, an iron wood-burning stove and an electric light. They had no bathroom, no running water, and no wood for the stove.

Our father recounted: "Soldiers guarded us with machine guns. They said it was for our own protection from people who might come in to harm us, but the guns were pointed at us, not at anything outside the fence. It began to get cold and we had no tools to cut wood. They paid us from sixteen dollars to nineteen dollars a month, depending on the jobs we held in camp, and we used that money to buy two-man saws, axes, and splitting wedges. Winter came, and it got pretty miserable until those tools came, and we could get some wood cut."

Dave and Ed were born in the Rohwer camp, delivered in makeshift medical facilities by internee physicians. Mom recalled nights during her pregnancies when she would have to walk through the mud to the community bathhouse. She and everyone else in camp had to use military-style, un-partitioned showers and toilets. Meals were served military style at a community dining hall. There was also a laundry facility on each of the thirty-six groups of barracks called blocks. Amid these conditions, the internees worked to provide services for their small city of 9,000. They served as teachers, doctors, nurses, mechanics, and cooks. Some locals outside the camp thought we were being coddled by the government because they gave us shelter and food. It was hardly a dream—more of a nightmare.

Our family lived in these conditions for nearly three years, until July 1945 when the internees were released. We, and tens of thousands of other Japanese Americans being released from the camps, faced a daunting question: what now? Mom and Dad had nothing left in California, and word was that many Californians were unfriendly to the returning Japanese Americans. There was open hostility, even shootings. Many of the internees in Arkansas were intent on staying in the Midwest, possibly settling in Chicago, but some heard that the people in St. Louis were friendly and would welcome them. Our father—we called him "Pop"—soon received three job offers from St. Louis companies to repair radios. Our parents decided to move us here. We were among around 300 internees from the camp who made our way to St. Louis to start over.

Mom and Pop were diminutive in stature, but strong authority figures to us. They came from simple farming backgrounds and although they had limited education, they were resourceful at what they did. Pop learned electronics by taking correspondence courses while in the internment camp and, by necessity, Mom became a skilled seamstress and patternmaker. As little kids, we saw our father as an imposing, firm disciplinarian. Years later, we came to realize that this five-foot-tall figure was simply hardworking, disciplined, and dedicated with high moral values and standards—he expected the same from us. Pop was always busy at work or on home projects. Mom was the main influence on us and managed to pass on her key values with stories from her family and youth that we still remember. She had a strong sense of community, participation, and giving back. Both were quiet and reserved in a very Japanese way.

Growing up in St. Louis in the fifties and sixties was about the same for us as it was for most kids in our neighborhood at that time. We knew that we looked different but were treated just like anyone else. We had just come out of World War II in which Japan was the enemy. All our friends were Caucasian, and we did our best to become Americanized in the postwar times. We didn't speak Japanese at home. Mom and Pop made a conscious effort to ensure their children spoke without accents to aid in our acceptance. In hindsight, they traded off cultural identity for community acceptance. Years ago, actor Goro Suzuki changed his Japanese name to Jack Soo in order to assume a Chinese persona. Politician Norman Mineta once said that he sat in front of a mirror practicing holding his eyes open wide in order to look less Asian. Growing up, the three of us worked hard in sports and scholastics and were accepted and well thought of in the community, as were most of the other Japanese American families. Since the Japanese American families who relocated into the St. Louis area were widely scattered, individual families became more assimilated into their respective communities.

Despite everything our families gave up to be accepted, we still found ways to hold on to pieces of Japanese culture. We remember the first Japanese Festivals as simple events with food and music. They were held in church basements or parking lots. Food, including familiar Japanese finger foods and other fare, was enjoyable; however, an added attraction at the Japanese Festivals was entertainment such as group Japanese folk dancing and "talent" shows. One year, Dick remembers, a young Japanese American visitor, dressed in his US Army uniform, reluctantly sang the Hank Williams song, "Jambalaya" to the accompaniment of a scratchy 78 rpm record player. Socializing with young friends and playing tag with them was always great fun for us youngsters. These gatherings were organized by the Japanese American Citizen's League (JACL), funded by the St. Louis chapter's expenses, and included social activities such as Easter egg hunts,

Fourth of July picnics, Christmas parties, and potluck dinners with a Japanese movie. The JACL became the uniting organization for the Japanese American community in St. Louis. JACL activities included civic, cultural, and social events including their sole fund-raising event, their Fall Festival.

In the early 1960s, JACL's focus became broader and increased in scope from the Japanese American community, culminating in a commitment to make a gift of appreciation to the people of St. Louis. Our families had come a long way from the days in the camp, and St. Louis played a large role in that story. The city was the foundation on which we rebuilt our lives. Among other ideas, the local JACL board proposed a small Japanese garden—a physical manifestation of the culture our families kept alive despite the pressure after the war, and one that would live on for future generations. They believed a garden would symbolically embody Japanese culture, keep it alive in St. Louis, and educate people in a city where diversity is often a binary matter.

In the early seventies, JACL's George Hasegawa found an interested partner in the Missouri Botanical Garden. With the Garden committed to building a Japanese Garden, the St. Louis JACL located a landscape architect, UCLA Professor Koichi Kawana, and funded the initial plans for the garden. Support from the Botanical Garden's director, Dr. Peter Raven, and the design from respected Professor Kawana brought the fourteen-acre garden into being. Funding came from generous contributions from individuals, foundations, and institutions. Government grants proved to be instrumental and necessary to create a garden of this magnitude.

The first festival held at the Missouri Botanical Garden four decades ago, in 1976, was "more like a picnic than anything," older brother Dick recalls, but it brought in 10,000 people. Organizers of the early festivals included Hasegawa, Anna Crosslin, George Sakaguchi, and Sam Nakano. They organized many demonstrations including dance, kite making, origami, martial arts, and music. There were exhibits of samurai swords, dolls, flower arrangements, kimonos, bonsai, and pottery. There was home cooking by ladies in the JACL. The Japanese garden and festival are now among the largest in the United States.

Thus, Japanese Garden and Japanese Festival are realizations of the dream of the St. Louis Japanese American community. They are gifts to the people of St. Louis for their kindness when our families arrived from the dark days of the internment camps, and many of us remain involved not only to honor our parents, but to thank the people of St. Louis ourselves. It's a massive endeavor to take on each year, but one we take on with pride.

As Dave said during one of those brief moments of calm leading up to the 2018 festival: "From their humble beginnings on a strawberry farm in California, through the internment camp in Arkansas, to contributing to the creation of this garden in St. Louis, Mom and Pop would be pleased and proud of what they helped accomplish here."

After the Holocaust, St. Louis Was Home

MIRIAM MORRIS

In no country in the world can we feel happier, freer, and more joyful than in the USA. —David Friedmann

We were a unit—my mother Hildegard, my father David, and me, Miri. My parents were Jewish Holocaust survivors who married in 1948 Prague. One year later they fled communist Czechoslovakia for Israel, where I was born. In November 1954, the Friedmann family boarded the SS *Jerusalem* to New York with thirty borrowed dollars to begin life in a new country. Besides the typical baggage of immigrants, we brought something unique—a trunk packed with artwork created after my father's liberation from Nazi concentration camps.

David Friedmann was born in 1893 in Mährisch Ostrau, Austria-Hungary (today Ostrava, Czech Republic). He studied etching with Herman Struck and painting with Lovis Corinth in Berlin. He achieved acclaim as a painter known for his portraits drawn from life and became a leading press artist of the 1920s, sketching hundreds of celebrated personalities including Albert Einstein, Arnold Schoenberg, Emanuel Lasker, and Thomas Mann. His flourishing career was prematurely terminated in 1933 by the Nazi regime. As each of his options narrowed, he continued to produce art illustrating the events and personal experiences of his time. In 1938, he fled with his first family to Prague, escaping from the Nazis with only his artistic talent as a means to survive. He depicted human fate as a refugee in Prague, as a prisoner in the Lodz Ghetto, in the Auschwitz sub-camp Gleiwitz I, and as a survivor. His wife Mathilde and little daughter Mirjam Helene perished. Nazi authorities looted his left-behind art in Berlin and Prague.

My mother, Hildegard Taussig, was born in 1921 in Berlin. Until the Nazis came to power in 1933, her family lived happily in Gleiwitz, Upper Silesia—Germany at the time. The increasing persecution of Jews forced their escape to Prague. However, the terror followed with Germany's occupation of Czechoslovakia in 1939. Hilda's older sister Else fled to Palestine. The family was further torn apart in 1941 when my mother and her father Karl were deported to the Theresienstadt Ghetto. They survived several camps, but Hilda never saw her mother, Irma, or twin sister, Ingeborg, ever again.

My parents met in January 1946, in Český Dub, a town near Prague, where my mother helped my father hang his first Holocaust art exhibition. The collection grew and came to the attention of high-ranking communist officials who wanted his art for the war museum. After my parents wed in May 1948, my father planned not only their escape to Israel, but also the rescue of his work. I was born in 1950, when Israel was still a new state in poor economic circumstances. Undeterred by his sixty-one years, my father set his ambitions on America.

My father had to forget what was hidden in his heart, the paintings from the concentration camps, and focus on his family's future. Straight from the boat he auditioned for General Outdoor Advertising Company, Inc.—billboards. My father painted as fast as he could because only this would save us from poverty. GOA did not care about his age or that he barely spoke English. They were impressed with an accomplished artist who painted with astonishing speed—the same skill that saved his life years prior. In 1944 at Gleiwitz I, he had improvised with primitive materials, making his own paints and brushes out of camp supplies, to paint a mural across a barrack's wall to show the SS officers his artistic ability and spare him from death. Staring at the blank wall, he thought of the Havel River he once painted in Berlin, "with a blue sky and white clouds, with trees and small red-roofed houses between, water and white sailboats reflecting on the water." He painted the scene fast, and was spared.

GOA moved us first to Chicago and then to St. Louis in February 1956. After only fifteen months in America, my father had achieved the top artist position at this branch. The opportunity gave him reason to believe there was still a place where his ability as a painter could be respected. The new career brought recognition and satisfaction with life in America, and the Friedmann family called St. Louis home. One Christmas, to the delight of his co-workers, my father performed a one-hour violin concert standing in a pickup truck in GOA's studio downtown.

As my mother and I went about town, we admired his gigantic billboards for companies, such as Hunt's Tomato Sauce, 7-Up soda, Budweiser, Michelob, and Falstaff beer. Instead of scenes depicting Nazi persecution of Jews as he had in Europe, he painted the iconic Budweiser Clydesdales and happy folks, selling beer on two-story tall billboards. As an adult, I wondered what my father thought as he painted hot dogs, beer, and salads—far removed from his old world.

By the age of five, I already sensed we were different. My parents and their friends had accents and I was aware they all bore tattooed numbers on their arms. An aura of indescribable sadness hung in the air as survivors tried to create happy homes in a foreign land for their children. Our family joined Congregation Shaare Emeth and the Jewish Community Centers Association (JCCA). My parents found the strength to rebuild their lives and raise me in an environment of love, learning, classical music, and art. However, at times sadness hovered like a thick gray cloud and would dissipate when I came around. We spoke German at home. When my parents did not want me to hear they spoke Czech.

I do not recall when I learned of my father's first daughter. My mother said, "You were named after your father's first child Mirjam Helene. He wanted so much to have another girl and was overjoyed when you were born and held you in his arms. This was the greatest day in his life." That there had been another "Miriam Friedmann" was an overwhelming thought to understand as a young child. My father was lucky to have retrieved photographs of his family and this is how I met his first wife Mathilde and their daughter Mirjam Helene, my half-sister. From their warm appearance, I could tell they had been a fine family. I never dared to ask him about his murdered family; it was too painful. I learned more about their experiences as an adult reading my father's diaries and testimony. Mirjam Helene was one of approximately 1.5 million Jewish children murdered during the Holocaust. The Holocaust was rarely discussed in front of us, the children of survivors. In fact, "Holocaust" was not even a term that was used. Instead, my parents and other survivors would say "KZ," pronounced "Ka-tset." In German, it's an abbreviation for *"konzentrationslager"*—concentration camp. Yet we children were aware who the survivors were—after all, most had numbers tattooed on their arms.

Usually, just the three of us celebrated holidays, but occasionally these were spent with the lovely Goldsmit family, whose parents were survivors from the Netherlands. My parents were elegantly dressed at these festive dinners and made hearty toasts with raised wineglasses—a picture of happiness shielding sadness for the loss of their families. Thanksgiving was extra special. My mother cooked an enormous turkey dinner and invited guests who also had found refuge in St. Louis. Often that guest was a man named Carl Stock, who had escaped Nazi Germany to Shanghai, China, where Jewish refugees lived in a ghetto. He didn't have a family, as far as I knew. As an adult, I researched Carl's life and learned he had been born in Berlin as Karl Klopstock. The only other details I found were that his mother was deported to the Riga Ghetto in Latvia and killed in 1942, and that in 1948 he traveled alone on a ship from Shanghai to San Francisco.

Growing up Jewish in St. Louis, I felt no different than anyone else. Like my parents, I had Jewish and non-Jewish friends; after all I attended a secular school and participated in related activities. Hamilton Elementary School was only a block from our first apartment at Westminster Place. I played with the kids who lived on my street, many of them children of survivors. Summers were spent at the JCCA day camp and later, sleepaway camp. Three weeks in the Ozarks was enough for me. I was happy to go home and to the solitude of reading a book. We enjoyed Heman Park Swimming Pool and picnics with my parents' survivor friends and their families. In 1956, I joined the Girl Scout Brownies as a first grader. The brown uniform outraged my father. He still pictured the detested Hitler Youth. My mother reminded my father this was America. I would learn good citizenship. In 1960, we became proud United States citizens and symbolically dropped the second "n" in Friedmann. Eventually, my parents were able to buy a home in University City.

In 1961, exciting news from Germany planted a seed for the future—one that would grow to uncover my father's buried history and work. In 1954, my father won restitution for art and property looted by the Gestapo in Berlin. It had taken seven years for the International Supreme Restitution Court in Berlin to adjudicate an upward adjustment. The *St. Louis Post-Dispatch* sent a reporter and photographer to interview my father, resulting in a spectacular full-page article with the headline: "Artist Who Had to Paint for His Life." I had a glimpse into my father's past and began to understand its importance.

We spent almost every Sunday at Forest Park—our go-to place, strolling through the zoo or art museum. We enjoyed picnics, long walks, and great times together. My father often took along his camera or sketch pad to capture the scenery. Crowds would gather to watch him sketch. In 1962, my father retired from commercial art. At the age of sixty-eight, he still had the artistic temperament and drive for self-expression and new challenges. One project developed into life studies of library patrons: *Enjoyment in Libraries with the Candid Pencil of David Friedman.* He traveled by bus from one library to another sketching one hundred portraits. Even in wintry weather, his enthusiasm for his work was unbounded. He roamed the streets, alleys, and parks to capture the sprawling city and titled the series, *Urban Scene.*

The library, the outdoors—these were my father's sanctuaries, his escape from graphic memories. However, the art hidden in his heart would not be silent. In the ghetto and concentration camp, my father's painting was an act of survival and a form of resistance. Now in St. Louis, he was compelled to impress upon the American consciousness to safeguard their democracy. His burning desire was to show to the world the ruthless persecution and inhumanity as practiced by the Nazis, in the hope that such barbarism would never happen again. My father wrote in a letter, "I wish everyone had to take a good look at the artwork. They have to look at what persecution under the Nazi regime was, and it can happen again, for in America to be a Nazi, to be a communist is not prohibited. Against an evil world I will work further and try to put my feelings down on canvas or paper against anti-Semitism, against race hatred of all people. My wife Hilda has the same opinion."

In his art, he bore witness to Nazi Germany's killing of innocents and called the series, *Because They Were Jews!* Scenes of hunger, forced labor, torture, murder, and the death march exploded over the paper. The exhibitions at St. Louis's Jewish Community Centers Associations in 1964 were among the first in the United States and created a sensation. My father supplemented his art with descriptions to create a singularly detailed pictorial and written record—a testament against hate and intolerance in all its many forms.

My father finished his last self-portrait in 1978, the same year Gerald Green's miniseries *Holocaust* launched on prime time television. This fictionalized drama was a commercial hit and brought a long dormant subject to the surface. It generated new interest and national discussions about the Holocaust. One of St. Louis's news stations learned about my father—a survivor living in St. Louis, who, like one of the characters in the movie, had been an artist in the camp. A reporter with a film crew in tow arrived at my parent's home. The sudden attention was much too late for my father. He was filled with emotion and could barely speak when questioned. Instead, my mother told their story and showed the art.

Soon after the newscast, a viewer named Elsie Shemin-Roth arrived at the Friedman house. Moved by the interview, Elsie asked to buy a painting so her children would never forget their heritage. My father was taken aback by the unexpected interest. She chose the painting of three Lodz Ghetto inmates with the yellow star sewn on their coats bearing the inscription "*Jude.*" Elsie took the painting home the same day. Years later, she donated the painting to the St. Louis Holocaust Museum and Learning Center, where it hangs in the permanent exhibition.

Lodz Ghetto Inmates. Tempera, 1945. From David Friedmann's series, *Because They Were Jews!*
Permanent Exhibition of the St. Louis Holocaust Museum and Learning Center.
Copyright ©1989 Miriam Friedman Morris

In 1980 my father died at the age of eighty-six. My mother continued to express their beliefs to guard against extremist groups who are a serious threat to our freedom. She spoke to schools and organizations with an emphasis to be kind to our neighbors across cultures. We teamed up to exhibit my father's art and donated a selection to the United States Holocaust Memorial Museum in Washington, D.C. After my mother's death in 1989, I carried my parents' message forward. I donated a drawing of city hall to University City in my parents' memory and in gratitude to the town where we lived in tranquility. The framed drawing hangs among other historic documents in city hall, where the mayor declared the first David Friedman Day on April 30, 2007.

David and Hilda Friedman emerged from the destruction of the Holocaust with the passion to live, and found a welcome and safe haven in St. Louis. Watching them, I learned courage, tenacity, and the knowledge to never to give up your dreams. And most inspiring and extraordinary was my father's resilience to begin again, to create a new family and reproduce the haunting images and traumatic memories of the Holocaust. He is recognized internationally with works displayed in the permanent exhibitions of the Holocaust History Museum, Yad Vashem, Jerusalem, the Sokolov Museum, Czech Republic, and the St. Louis Holocaust Museum and Learning Center.-Further, his works are in the collections of museums and libraries in St. Louis, Cleveland, Washington, D.C., New York, Israel, the Czech Republic, Germany, the Netherlands, as well as the Auschwitz-Birkenau State Museum in Poland. Fascination with my father's Nazi-looted art launched a four-decade journey across three continents to find works and uncover the mysteries of his life spanning pre-World War I Germany, through to post-World War II Czechoslovakia, Israel, and the United States. I collect and organize his art, facilitate exhibitions, lecture, and write—and hope to add more pieces to the mosaic of my father's legacy.

In 2012, I received a phone call from St. Louis. On the other end of the line was a man named Maurice Wichmann. He introduced himself as an acquaintance of my parents, and was the owner of the *Yemenite Jewish Beggar* piece my father had painted in the 1950s when we lived in Israel. My father had created a series of paintings of Yemenite Jews in Israel, sympathetic to the plight of the impoverished people emigrating from Yemen during those years. I knew this particular painting well—the man's long white beard hanging to his chest, eyes downcast and brow furrowed, a small cup in his hand—but only from a black and white photo displayed in my father's album. Soon after, Maurice sent a color photo of the piece to add to the collection. Once I saw the painting in color, I realized that my father had painted himself into the background of the scene.

Maurice wasn't even Jewish. He was Catholic, and had bought the painting years prior, simply because he liked it. To this day, I am not only touched that Maurice cared so much to find me, but am continuously astounded by, and proud of, how my parents' legacy continues to reach people around the world—from Europe, to Israel, to St. Louis.

When Departing

MAJA SADIKOVIC

The drivers were calling
for us to load
the buses. We entered and
my little daughter walked
down the aisle finding a seat on
the right side, somewhere in the middle
so she could wave
goodbye to grandma and
grandpa out of the window.
She sat down and
immediately leaned on
the window of the bus.
The bus loaded
a little while and
then finally the doors
closed shut. We were
leaving. We were leaving and going into places
unknown. I'm watching through the window with
her and watching my city
get left behind, watching my mother-in-law stay
intact but out. She just stood
there as if buried in the concrete in the sidewalk, hands
crossed across her chest, watching her
granddaughter, with the hottest
tears streaming down. Her little
blond granddaughter was leaving
her, and my father-in-law shaking his head in disbelief—

Maja—turn to grandma and grandpa and
blow them a big kiss.

She did and then
turned to me saying
how grandma
was crying.

No honey, grandma just got sun in her eyes.

My chest felt
the weight of an airless space, pressing
my breasts
back, wrapping my ribs
in a hundred
barbed wires, its own shrapnel cage.

A Refugee Family's Pursuit of Happiness in St. Louis

VENETA RIZVIC

Most kids don't have very vivid memories of their first day in the second grade, but I do.

It was the first time I stepped into a classroom where I didn't understand the language spoken by my classmates and teacher. It was the first time I had ever seen an African American or Hispanic person. That can be overwhelming for a seven-year old.

Just a few weeks before that, I stepped foot in St. Louis for the first time in my life with parents who had only ever left their native country to live in refugee camps to escape war.

Sometimes stories like that sound surreal, like they couldn't have possibly happened to anyone. Looking back on it now, it still feels hard to believe that it all happened to me.

I landed at St. Louis Lambert International Airport on September 2, 1998. I was greeted by my uncle, who I hadn't seen in a few years because he left for the United States straight from the refugee camp we were living in a couple of years prior. He's also the uncle that first brought the news to us of my dad getting shot during the war. He's also the uncle who sponsored us as refugees and supported us, financially and emotionally, following the culture shock we felt our first few weeks in St. Louis.

St. Louis wasn't always home. My parents and I had been forced out of our home in Velika Kladusa, Bosnia and Herzegovina, several times during the war that led to the breakup of Yugoslavia and resulted in millions of displaced families in the early to mid-1990s. The first time was in 1994, when I was just three years old. We stayed in the Turanj refugee camp in Karlovac, Croatia, which borders Velika Kladusa. Turanj was basically no-man's-land, between Croat and Serb enemy lines. The area was riddled with mines, which meant I didn't spend much time playing with other children outside. We lived there for four months and returned home after. That didn't last very long because our home became too dangerous again. My parents feared that staying there would result in capture or death.

Time becomes a blur when you're always on the run or fearing for your life. Sometime in 1995, we made our way to another refugee camp in Croatia. This camp was called Kupljensko, and it's where I attended preschool—if you want to call it that. Our preschool class was housed in a tent and we ate stale slices of bread with jam on them, when we had jam. If we didn't have it, we simply ate the stale slices of bread.

It was sometime between our stays in those refugee camps that my dad was shot. I remember that we were at home in Velika Kladusa when my uncle came home to deliver the news. Soldiers were sometimes allowed to come home from time to time to visit with family, depending on where they were stationed, which is how my uncle was able to come home and tell us about my dad.

My uncle's fateful visit home is one of my first memories as a kid in Velika Kladusa. Our house was on top of a hill and I remember playing outside and seeing my uncle making his way home. I ran down the hill to meet him, as I had dozens of times before. When he got close, he scooped me up in his arms. It was in that moment that I knew something was wrong. He didn't typically pick me up. He always just took my hand and walked back to the house with me.

The bullet that hit my dad in Velika Kladusa in March of 1995 entered his head on the left side of his forehead and came out from his right temple, shattering that side of his skull. Unlike thousands of others who were killed during the Bosnian War, my dad lived. But to this day, he has some handicaps due to the bullet that nearly killed him and kept him in a wheelchair for a couple of years. He had extensive nerve damage and he can't feel much of anything on the left side of his body, like a punch in the arm or a scratch on his leg, though he can walk and perform most day-to-day tasks. He can speak and he even drives.

It was because of my dad's medical problems that we decided to pursue a life in the United States. It was also because a normal and successful life in Velika Kladusa after the war ended was not possible. There were no jobs and it seemed like there was no future.

The process of becoming a refugee in the United States is a long and excruciating one. The entire process took about a year for us, but it can take up to two years or more for some. After we filled out that initial application, my parents were put through extensive interviews, not once, but twice. I had to be present for the interviews but wasn't questioned like my parents. After the interviews, we were all put through a health checkup, and after quite a bit of poking and prodding, we were finally given the OK to move to the US.

The day we landed at St. Louis Lambert International Airport was the day my life changed forever. And I'll forever be grateful to St. Louis for that.

When I started the second grade at Hodgen Elementary School, it was both the scariest and most exciting time in my life. The students and teachers that I encountered during my first year in school are part of the reason that I have succeeded in life. My classmates took it upon themselves to teach me new words daily. I was even named a line leader in the spring of my second grade year. That was probably the proudest moment of my first school year in America.

Fast forward twenty years and I have accomplished many of the goals my parents set out for me when they decided to move us across the globe. I graduated from Affton High School in 2009, where I was part of the track and field team and a member of the National Honor Society and the student council. I was fortunate enough to attend and graduate from my dream college—the University of Missouri in Columbia. Nothing compares to my parents' faces the day I walked across that stage. Since graduating from Mizzou, I have worked as a journalist in Cedar Rapids, Iowa, and now in my hometown of St. Louis.

I can't sit here and tell you about the number of people I've seen get shot, or blown up, or die in front of my eyes, because I was lucky enough not to see those atrocities. Or maybe I'm just lucky that I was so little and can't remember experiencing them. But I can't say the same for my parents. I can see the pain in their eyes every time we talk about the war or every time we go back to Bosnia for a visit.

But more importantly, after all of these years, I can now see the happiness in their eyes as well, thanks to the fact that we were able to move here so many years ago.

I remember the day all three of us finally became citizens of the United States of America. It was one of the proudest days of our lives. I remember attending my first Cardinals game, my first Rams game, and my first Blues game—all unimaginable when we were living in our war-torn country—but thanks to the generosity of the US and St. Louis, they are among our best memories. Though visiting the Gateway Arch is something I do on a regular basis as a reporter today, I'll never forget the first time I visited the monument. I'll always remember the first time I ate toasted ravioli, Imo's Pizza, and Ted Drewes.

Outside of our American experiences in St. Louis, there were parts that felt like Bosnia, too. When I was in middle school, I joined a traditional Bosnian folklore dance group. I loved being able to connect to my birthplace in this way. I grew up with several Bosnian friends because the community in St. Louis grew quickly. Today, there are more than 60,000 Bosnians in St. Louis, making it the largest Bosnian community outside of Bosnia itself. The Bevo Mill neighborhood is now also known as "Little Bosnia," and St. Louis has even been called "Sarajevo West."

Though most Bosnians in St. Louis have found some form of success, the war's impact is still visible, even after all these years. Others have continued to struggle. Trauma left over from the war, combined with the multiple jobs that most parents juggle once moving here, leaves little time for families to spend time together. This has led to violence and drug abuse among some in the community. The Bosnian community is a proud one. We've gone through a lot, and it's hard for some families to admit that they've escaped war only to have their family members succumb to drugs.

But there are the moments that remind us that all the struggles were worth it.

I got married in September 2017—something I think was unimaginable for my parents at one point in our lives. My husband, who is also Bosnian, and I got married at the Magic House in Kirkwood and we served dinner from the Pasta House to our guests (you can't get anymore St. Louis than that). Both Bosnian and American friends of our families attended our wedding, which was a testament to how far we had come in our twenty years in St. Louis. It felt like we had finally come full circle.

Dear Father

IBRO SULJIC

Dear father,
I am grateful to have called you that
I miss the days I was younger, back then I used to call you dad
We came to this country and for our family you'd break your back
But these were the days our family was still intact
See, you're the reason why I am a successful person, a man
You used to tell me right from wrong, you would make me understand
the struggles that you been through before America the Great
We didn't know people here would do nothing but be jealous and hate
I remember coming here living in Rockford, Illinois,
Wearing donated clothes and playing with anything as a toy
Food stamps was a blessing we used to walk to the grocery store
Come back with two full cars like we never ate before
You couldn't find a job and others' trash became our gold
I remember you riding your bike with a broken TV on your shoulders home
You would fix it and I never doubted you for a second
As a young age of nine, dad, I got the message
You would think life would get to a place of peace
I remember asking god at times to help my family please
Never could put myself in your pain and in your shoes
The day that you found out about mom leaving I saw it just breaking you
The struggles that you went through just battling your own self
I wish I could have helped you instead of that bottle on the shelf
But I knew how you were because we are built the same
You lost the person that you loved and worse you felt ashamed
I just wish that you were here and your life didn't end so soon
Because no matter what ever happened you were the greatest man I ever knew
So Rest in Peace, dad, I love you and I'll never be the same
I wish you're in a better place now and I will see you soon again

Pilgrim on the Interstate

NARTANA PREMACHANDRA

I awoke in a state of shock on Thursday, March 5, 2015.

Even though I was prepared for the events of that day, the full, daunting significance of what was about to happen only revealed itself to me as I entered waking consciousness that morning.

"From this day forward," I thought, sitting up on my bed, "I will no longer have access to a Cadillac."

It was true. After forty-six years of having my father's Cadillac always at the ready to take me where I needed to go, I would no longer have access to that glorious icon of American engineering, creativity, and radiant, no-excuse panache. We were selling it today.

My father had died the previous December, unexpectedly; and while we would've love to have kept his car, it was simply not practical.

Even though I had driven his car now and then, I never felt comfortable driving such a big car for daily errands. As my Chilean friends put it, when they sat inside the comfortable vehicle for the very first time, "It's like a living room in here."

Plus, we couldn't afford all the expenses that went along with keeping the car—auto insurance and property tax, two of the banes of keeping a car of one's own. Not to mention, of course, upkeep.

And thirdly—and perhaps most significantly—this 2007 Cadillac DTS was *his*. Ever since he bought his first car of the legendary lineage in 1964—a Cadillac DeVille, with a body sleek, long, and black (and bearing a modified tail fin)—he always drove Cadillacs.

My dad drove that fine car constantly, as he picked up blood specimens from doctors' clinics to analyze in his thyroid specialty lab in south St. Louis County. One of his clinics was in St. Peters, a good half-hour outside of St. Louis, across the Missouri River. He went there twice or thrice a week for years; I used to wonder when his weekly pilgrimages to St. Peters would end. While he was an expert driver, I naturally worried a bit about him as he grew older.

In the end, his weekly rounds to St. Peters ended in a way I'd never imagine.

My mother arrived in the United States on November 22, 1963. The day John F. Kennedy was shot.

She heard the news before my dad, in what was still Idlewild Airport in New York City. My dad had gone to claim their baggage. A woman from the Philippines was seated in a chair next to her, crying. She too had just arrived in the United States, and it seemed as if she already missed her homeland.

My mother noticed an outburst of chatter. Then someone pasted a piece of paper on the wall:

President Kennedy has been assassinated.

She told my father who didn't believe her; he thought it was a joke in poor taste.

Later, my dad, a medical researcher specializing in the endocrine system, who went to his lab seven days a week, who worked until a few days before he died, who believed wholeheartedly in the fail-safe formula of faith, prayer, and hard work, stayed home from his lab to watch President Kennedy's funeral on the television.

On his desk still sits a plaque: "Ask not what your country can do for you, but what you can do for your country."

Not only did my dad contribute greatly to pure science—researching the thyroid gland and the endocrine system and their relations to diabetes and aspects of gerontology, among other avenues of interest—he and my mother began a classical Indian dance company, Dances of India, in 1977. It celebrated its fortieth season in 2017-2018. This is a milestone for a minority arts company in the Midwest.

As anyone in the arts knows, you can't "plan" for your dance company—or your film, or your novel—to break through, gain respect from the community, and be around for decades. My mother once said, reflecting upon four decades of leading the premier classical Indian dance company in St. Louis, "It just happened."

That's the thing about destiny—it just happens. For I'm certain that when my dad came to the US, he never imagined that in between his trips to his lab, he'd drive his family around for dance performances—not simply around St. Louis and Missouri, but as far afield as New York City. It is hard to believe now, but in the 1980s there weren't enough Indian performing arts companies in NYC to participate in a Festival of India, so the organizers invited us to come. And we did—in Dad's Cadillac.

But my dad didn't consider driving his wife, daughter, and students around the country a hassle.

Why not? Certainly, he had developed a deep respect for dance since marrying my mother. He had never been exposed to dance in his own family; once he saw my mother perform Bharata Natyam, he realized how much dedication and discipline it took to not simply learn this traditional art, but to perfect it.

But there was another reason. It's the reason he—this soft-spoken South Indian scientist—treasured his Cadillac.

He loved to drive.

And he loved the interstates. He drove across wide swaths of America without a cellphone or GPS for decades. Once, he told me, his tire blew out somewhere in Missouri—I think—and he landed in a ditch. From then on, he learned how to maneuver the car carefully for any eventuality.

He first arrived in North America in 1958, soon after the Federal Aid Highway Act of 1956 was signed, inaugurating the birth of the interstate. His life here developed alongside the establishment—not just the dream, but the *manifestation*—of the eternal road. As President Eisenhower put it, in a speech in Cadillac Square, Michigan, in 1954:

> We are pushing ahead with a great road program, a road program that will take this Nation out of its antiquated shackles of secondary roads all over this country and give us the types of highways that we need for this great mass of motor vehicles. It will be a nation of great prosperity, but will be more than that: it will be a nation that is going ahead every day.

I can only wonder at the excitement my dad felt, arriving in the United States at such an exhilarating point in time, a time when the country was doing all it could to expand one's frontiers.

How much did my dad love his Cadillac? He loved it so much he once shipped it to India in the 1960s to show to his relatives. My grandmother wrote in her journal, "Oh boy! It was a sensation when the car passed thru on the roads . . . the policeman at the circle instead of giving signals would get stunned and stand in a rigid pose."

The Cadillac—chariot of Marilyn Monroe and Jackie O., muse of Elvis Presley and Bruce Springsteen—was now a traveling home for a family of South Indian Iyengar Brahmins from Bangalore, a town of which few in the United States had ever heard.

How could they have heard of Bangalore, when they had barely heard of India?

As I was growing up in the 1970s and 1980s in St. Louis, my family and I often received the question, "Where are you from?" And every time we said we were Indian, or even that we were from India, well, that was a mistake. For people—men and women, young and old—always, *always* responded excitedly, saying, "Really? I'm a quarter-Cherokee!"

Sometimes we just laughed it off and didn't say anything, and sometimes, we tried to emphasize that no, we were *from a country called India*, which didn't necessarily clarify the confusion caused by Chris Columbus's colossal error of geography. Once in a while, however, when the fog did lift, we'd receive responses along the lines of, "Wow. India. It must be hot there." Or, "India. Wow. Do you do belly dancing?"

Three months before he died, my dad told my cousin he was faced with a quandary—his Cadillac needed to be traded in, but he didn't like any of the new models.

I don't blame him; the newer models just don't have the élan that makes a Cadillac a Cadillac. Perhaps it was a sign. The world had changed too much. It was time to leave.

In the end, I was the one who went to his clinic in St. Peters for the last time. It was an ending to his pilgrimage I never imagined.

That morning, my dad was at home with the flu and, we would find out, pneumonia and bronchitis. He had never been sick in his life. I went to work. My mom had just had knee surgery and was in the hospital.

My stomach sank when I returned home. The house was completely dark. I ran inside. My dad was okay, just fast asleep. He had slept all day.

That night I went to St. Peters for him. We were sure he'd be back to work in a few days.

It was raining heavily as I set out on the highway. After I picked up the samples, I got back in the car to turn around and go home, and at that moment he called me, in the middle of his exhaustion, just to make sure I wasn't lost.

It was a dark, rainy night for a girl to be out on the highway alone, after all.

The first person to enter our house the morning after my dad died was Amos, a maintenance supervisor at the VA Hospital at the edge of Jefferson Barracks National Cemetery, where my dad had a laboratory for thirty years. Amos, blond-haired, blue-eyed, with a sweet smile, worked on every aspect of our home for more than thirty-five years—from the sump pump down below to the roof up above.

He came over that morning because we had set up an appointment with him, a week earlier, to do some work around the house.

I told him my dad died. He couldn't speak. He just hugged me. He later was interested in buying my dad's Cadillac, "because it's Doc's." But it just didn't happen. He did do, however, a lot more work for us, and became very protective of my mother and me.

Fourteen months to the day that I gave Amos the news of my dad's passing, there was a knock at our door.

I opened it. Amos's son.

"Dad's gone."

I was so shocked I had to sit down. Amos was only sixty-one.

Looking back on these events I can't help but feel, that somehow, the Harley-Davidson riding, tattooed Amos and my Cadillac driving, shirt-and-tie adorned dad, were connected deeply. As Amos's son told me, "They were like brothers."

In St. Louis County, I-170 ends. A mile before it does, there is a sign that strikes me with amazement and a *frisson* of fear: ALL VEHICLES MUST EXIT.

I can't believe that a grand majestic interstate can end.

But it does.

But hey, if I look hard enough, I can see Amos and my dad speeding off the interstate, away into the infinite on a Harley and a Cadillac. Nothing would please either one of them more.

And that's something to dance about.

A version of "Pilgrim on the Interstate" was first published in Panorama.

Finding Bethesda

MARK LOEHRER

In November of 1957, Hubert and June Schwartzentruber, a young newlywed couple from Ontario, moved into Pruitt-Igoe.

The Schwartzentrubers arrived to take the place of James and Rowena Lark as the Larks sought to retire from the Mennonite mission they had established the year before. A Pruitt-Igoe building bulletin for tenants of building C-15 East announced the news: "We will miss Rev. James and Rowena Lark greatly but are very fortunate to have with us now in Apt 906, Rev. Hubert and June Schwartzentruber. We welcome them to our building and hope that their stay with us will be an enjoyable one."

Hubert and I talk regularly on the phone. When I asked him how he thought Lark judged him upon arrival in St. Louis, he was sure Lark was disappointed. He felt the senior churchman viewed the young couple as out of place in the black ghetto, and felt that Hubert wouldn't amount to much as a pastor. In fact, in his report to the church leaders upon his departure from St. Louis, Lark recommended the Schwartzentrubers keep themselves occupied in the white Igoe apartments in order to build a mission there and spread the word, so that the tenants of Pruitt and Igoe might come together as brothers undivided by race. Hubert found this amusing but unsurprising. Later in life, he said, the two men became good friends.

A young reporter for the *St. Louis Globe-Democrat*, Ted Schafers, heard rumbles of the new arrivals possibly from contacts at the Housing Authority. Seen as an opportunity to broadcast the presence of the new mission, James Lark arranged for the reporter to meet with the young couple. On December 22, 1957, the *Globe-Democrat* ran a small piece: "Missionary Couple First White Residents in Pruitt Project." Schwartzentruber told Schafers of the hospitality and warmth the couple had received from neighbors, stating they felt as if they were treated as equals and that the black residents didn't seem to be as race conscious as whites in the city.

The publicity brought letters from around St. Louis.

"Let me take this opportunity to first explain my position, I am not of the Mennonite faith and fashion myself proud of my Orthodox Jewish faith," opened the letter from Bill Wilensky, owner of Globe Shoes at 2713 Franklin Avenue. Wilensky continued, "it felt good to read about your work and I am behind you in your attempts to bring about better relations among black and whites in St. Louis." Wilensky noted that while he was too timid to live among those with darker skin, the patrons of his business were almost entirely black, and thus he returned the favor by hiring exclusively black employees, both front and back of the house. He concluded by offering Hubert's family and the newly established Bethesda Mennonite congregation 10 percent off all purchases for the year of 1958.

"You say they treat you as 'equals'? IS THAT GOOD?" So read a line from a second letter the Schwartzentrubers received. "We can remember what our city was before these hordes poured up here from the South." Unsigned, this letter questioned how a white couple from a country that itself was almost entirely white could possibly hope to relocate into an area of St. Louis where the concentration of black residents approached 100 percent.

It was a question that did not elude the Schwartzentrubers themselves when they first moved to St. Louis. Who were they to impose their belief system on a people they had never known?

In his memoir, Hubert recounts the thoughts going through the young couple's mind when they moved into the projects. Having grown up in rural Ontario, neither June nor Hubert had many previous interactions with blacks of any nationality: "We were interested in staying physically alive. To stay alive we needed to make friends quickly with those with whom we shared the same elevator. And we had to make friends on their terms and not ours. They did not invite us to come. We invaded their territory. It became important for us to work toward trust relationships so that we would receive an invitation from the community to stay."

As time passed in the projects, the couple did make friends, largely through the church, which held Bible studies and children's club meetings in the couple's apartment. Families such as the Grays, Hudsons, and Mellingers became close friends of the Schwartzentrubers during their residence at the projects. Hubert is adamant that, as strangers, they didn't have the luxury of choosing friends. But through dinner gatherings, rides to the countryside, and day trips to the park, the Schwartzentrubers cultivated lasting relationships. Today he is firm, were he given a chance to do it again, there could be no possible route through St. Louis without living in Pruitt-Igoe.

He doesn't pretend that life was easy, for his family or any other, living in the projects. June Schwartzentruber had been born with a heart defect. The reality of life in the projects, where elevators only stopped on even number floors (they lived on the ninth) was unpleasant from the start. Hubert talks of other realities such as the ill-lit corridors and stairways they had to traverse, oftentimes stumbling over junkies hiding in the corners.

Worse still, and all too common, was being trapped in an elevator during a routine breakdown. Elevators, Hubert recalls, were often used as toilets by children, making the hours spent trapped in a broken elevator all the more worse.

Still, the couple and the ministry persisted. Progress moved about rapidly through 1958 as the congregation continued to slowly gain in numbers and weekly offerings. In June of that year, the church formally purchased a building at 2823 Dayton Street, just blocks away from the project. At two and a half stories, the building, purchased for the price of $4,500, offered a place for worship as well as apartments above and an unfinished basement that offered the possibility for classrooms. Seeking ways to boost the programming and staff of the young church, Hubert reached out to Elkhart, anticipating assistance through the recruitment of Voluntary Service units. In the 1960s, most of Bethesda's VS volunteers were couples straight out of college. Many of the men were conscientious objectors. In lieu of military service, these young couples worked in the inner city, including St. Louis, usually in fields of education, medicine, and social work. Those that arrived in St. Louis, such as the Gehmans (1961-1963) or the Hershbergers (1964-1966), worked with Bethesda directing Bible school, summer camps, and many other programming options that provided enrichment and recreation outlets to children of the projects they would otherwise not have enjoyed. Beginning in 1959 the church's Bible school attracted seventy-five pupils. In 1961, that number would swell to more than 325.

Helen Robinson, longtime Pruitt-Igoe resident and member of Bethesda (dating to her 1959 baptism) told me the attraction for most to the Mennonite mission was its accessibility: "The church succeeded because it operated from a perspective of 'come as you are,' so for people of the projects who felt excluded from the Catholic or Methodist churches because they lacked a nice pair of pants or a colorful dress to wear on Sunday morning, Bethesda offered us a doorway to the Lord."

She herself was first attracted to the church when she heard of it through her young children, who were themselves first introduced to the church programs by peers. Robinson was one of many who continued to attend the church after it moved to the Dayton address, while remaining in Pruitt-Igoe. Reflecting on Helen's words, Hubert wonders if his own approach to the pulpit was a factor in growing the congregation: "I didn't try to make everyone a Mennonite, I just tried to make them feel like they had somewhere to be safe and to have family."

In his memoir, Schwartzentruber is pointed in his criticism of those who would preach from behind the safety of the pulpit, be they in the suburbs or the inner city. The pulpit is a safe space. "No one ever held a gun to my face when I was behind the pulpit. But they did in the street. No one ever beat me to unconsciousness while in the pulpit but they did in the streets." Preaching at Bethesda inextricably changed Hubert's outlook. It brought him to a place where he often clashed, as vicious as Mennonites might, over theology. The theology of the streets versus the theology of the seminary.

"Preachers of the gospel speak empty words from the pulpit until they have practiced their theology in the streets," wrote Hubert in his memoir. It was a journey for him to get to this sentiment. He is unafraid to admit that he was tempted to remain behind a pulpit, but doubt lingered over whether he could be true to himself and his congregation by remaining apart from them.

This changed in the summer of 1965.

1965 was a gruesome year, both locally and across the nation. As fires and unrest roared in Watts, tensions were reaching a boiling point in St. Louis for similar reasons. In June of 1965, a minor, Melvin Cravens, who had been handcuffed on suspicion of theft, was shot dead by an officer while in custody of the city police department. Sporadic protests led by the NAACP and ACTION raged for the weeks following. As the summer drew to a close, another youth, Melvin Childs, only fifteen, was shot and killed by police fleeing from the scene of a suspected robbery in the Jeff Vander Lou neighborhood. Once again, the community organized.

"That was the day my path in St. Louis changed forever," Hubert told me. While he was in the church one afternoon preparing for the evening's activities, a neighborhood resident, who not a member of the church, walked in to speak with Hubert. His name was Macler Shepard.

In his memoir, Hubert recalls the moment Macler asked him to join the community on a march to city hall to protest police brutality: "All of a sudden my pulpit felt so safe. I did not want to march in the street. In fact, I even thought it was wrong to participate in the protest marches. The work of the pastor was to preach the gospel, what did marching with the tired and weary have to do with preaching the gospel?"

Hubert was faced with the decision of deciding to march or not. If he didn't march, he felt the community might see him as siding with "the oppressor." But, he cautioned, if he did go, he might march with unbelievers, an activity greatly frowned upon during his education in rural Ontario.

Worse, there might be communists present. Yet, he turned to Macler: "I told him, I will be there to march with you. . . . A congregation that does not reflect the voice of the community is, at best, a body struggling for survival and, at worst, the enemy of the truth."

Hubert has since retired, is nearing ninety years of age, and is living in a town about an hour north of Philadelphia. June, his wife with whom he lived with during his more than decade-long career in St. Louis, passed away in 1984 due to heart problems. One day in 2018, when I called to talk with him about his years in St. Louis, he was busy working away in his basement workshop. His second wife, Mary Rittenhouse Schwartzentruber, told me he stays active. Mary herself has a connection to St. Louis. She was a Summer VSer, part of a unit of volunteers dispatched to St. Louis each summer (though she only came twice) to assist the church. Following his departure from St. Louis, Hubert served the church as a member of the Mennonite Board of Congregational Ministries. He was active in a number of issues such as disarmament and civil rights.

Hubert relishes retelling the story of his first civil rights march on that fateful day in 1965. The community gathered in Jeff Vander Lou with a multigenerational crowd of around 300. The group included prominent leaders from organizations including the Nineteenth Ward Improvement Association (chaired by Macler Shepard), as well as representatives from CORE and ACTION, including Percy Green to Ivory Perry. And Hubert. And unbeknownst to Hubert, the newspapers reported the presence of a vocal contingent of communists from the W. E. B. Du Bois Club.

As the march approached a corner along Franklin Avenue, Hubert recalls a bartender from a corner pub leaning against the railing of his establishment's entrance. Sensing he had been seen, Hubert looked up to see the bartender, arm stretched out pointing directly at him, as he bellowed into the tavern, "Come and see everyone, look at this stupid preacher marching with them today."

To this day Hubert says there will never be a nicer compliment, or one he will treasure more, than that implied by the bartender. For him, it was a moment of clarity. He had found his place, his flock, and his calling.

His path forward would take him deep into neighborhood development as one of the co-founders of Jeff Vander Lou, Inc., a neighborhood development organization that captured headlines across the country with their innovative and successful assault on blight in the area around Bethesda Mennonite. But more impressive was his commitment to civil rights in the church itself. Often, he felt, those in Elkhart who were raised in rural towns were dismissive of the work being done by Mennonite missions in cities like St. Louis, Cleveland, and Saginaw.

When I asked him to explain, Hubert clarified, "it was a pretty violent community we were in and our traditional theology needed to be broadened; justice for the poor and downtrodden. I think I came to the conclusion [that] this was what Jesus was all about. He was restoring hope and courage to the poor, and that wasn't always accepted by our church leadership. They didn't have contact with the inner city poor."

Talking about the challenges of coming into urban ministry after being raised in a rural setting of Ontario, Hubert was forward with the obstacles that he, and other white Mennonite pastors, faced in their new surroundings: "All of us urban pastors in the early sixties came from communities much different than those we were preaching in, and we all struggled with our experiences—to unload our past for the new dynamics of the gospel—and that created some problems. Not everybody understood everybody else. If I could do it all over again, I would. I would hope I would do it a little better than I did the first time."

Still, he's adamant that the experience was worth it—the beatings, the contentious relationships with his brethren in the church, and his own day to day struggles with himself: "I know what it's like to be beaten to unconsciousness, and to come home to a house that was broken in. In spite of all of that, my feelings about ministry in the inner city is that that's where I felt most at home. I came from a farming community, as rural as rural could be, and yet I was immersed in St. Louis. There was a power beyond me to help me to survive."

Inside the Rent Strike of 1969

CAITLIN LEE AND CLARK RANDALL

"We know they are broke," Ed Roy Harris told reporters in late December, 1968, referring to the St. Louis Housing Authority. Harris lived in the Blumeyer Village public housing high-rises in near North City. "But we've gone to the state before. We've written letters. We've called—it didn't work," he told the *St. Louis Post-Dispatch*. "Politicians seem to respond to action."

Two weeks prior, Harris and other public housing tenants delivered a list of demands to city officials. Their demands countered a flurry of recent hikes in rents and were simple: lower the rent and treat us as human beings. Between 1965 and 1967, rent increases for public housing in St. Louis had ranged from 16 percent to 32 percent, depending on the project and the room count.

And Harris was right; the St. Louis Housing Authority was bottoming out. During the 1967-1968 fiscal year, the Authority recorded a deficit of well over $300,000. It had been a long time coming. Public housing projects across the country had been built with federal dollars, then left to be maintained by local rents. This financial structure, codified as law through the Federal Housing Act of 1937, often proved to be an ill fit for local implementation.

According to their 1968 budget, the St. Louis Housing Authority had a $54.16 allowance per unit, but operating costs totaled $57.38 per unit. This gap, stretched out over time and across the city's approximately 8,000 units, resulted in progressive underfunding and widespread deterioration of the housing units. The Housing Authority's deficit was compounded by increasing vacancy rates, themselves brought on in part by the deteriorating conditions of the units.

Tenants complained of rodent infestation, broken windows, lack of heating, and lack of repairs. Despite the substandard conditions, public housing tenants in St. Louis were at risk of being priced out of the city— out of their homes—by the rent increases.

The state of Missouri provided no relief, effectively clenching their purse. Through its cost of living calculations, the state estimated a minimum that residents needed "to live in health and dignity," but they provided households on welfare less than half of that amount. In 1968, the *St. Louis Post-Dispatch* called these payments "a disgrace." And public housing tenants in St. Louis were increasingly reliant on welfare to make ends meet: nearly two-thirds of tenants received welfare as their primary income. As rents rose and welfare stagnated, residents were spending 60 percent or more of their income on housing.

The St. Louis Housing Authority and the City of St. Louis witnessed this slow-motion train wreck and had been begging the state and federal governments for help for most of the 1960s.

"The whole public housing program is a federal program," Mayor Alfonso Cervantes said in 1968, "so they have a responsibility, regardless of what they say."

"And the state is responsible, too," he continued, "The state can't expect us to operate public housing when state welfare payments are so low that people have little or nothing left after they pay their rent."

"The projects," Cervantes finished, "have been heading towards bankruptcy for many years."

The city, nonetheless, refused to acknowledge the tenant's demands for several weeks.

The conditions at the Darst housing complex were reported to be some of the worst; the modernist high rise building of 645 units sat at Fourteenth and Park Avenue in the city's near south side. The building's condition, in line with the dwindling funds, was deteriorating. Tenants that could, left.

Jean King and her husband, who lived in Darst, were looking to move and had the means to do so. But as King later recalled, on her way to tour a new apartment building she saw a young girl from Darst picking a piece of bread up off the ground. Finding the girls' mother, King learned that the family's welfare payments had failed to adjust for their newborn child, leaving them in an overcrowded unit, having to make the impossible decision between paying for groceries or paying the rent. "Mrs. King, we don't have any food," King recalled being told.

King decided to stay at Darst. "Somebody's got to do something," King said, while at a meeting of tenants later that year. "I'm ready to go!" King became an organizer and was quickly recognized as a leader.

"We wish we could talk with Jean King," says Sunni Hutton. It is fall 2018, and Sunni is talking with her friend and co-organizer Shuron

Jones. "Gotta stay in touch with the old heads, you know?" They share a laugh—"The OG's."

The two are sitting at a sushi joint on Delmar. "This street ain't what it used to be," Shuron says. "The times I used to have down here, I'm telling you. 2008—it was different." Delmar Boulevard is the most infamous line of segregation in St. Louis; over the last decade it has turned from a hub for black culture into an extension of Washington University's campus. Plans for adding a ferris wheel were recently proposed.

The two recount the time they met a few summers back at St. Louis's Pride event. "Yes! The *black* Pride event!" Shuron clarifies.

"Child, it was hot, it was so hot, and we just danced," Sunni says, "We were the only people silly enough to be dancing in the middle of the street."

"It turned out you lived like three blocks from me," Sunni says. She started inviting Shuron to an area initiative called So Fresh So Clean, where residents pick up waste and encourage neighbors to recycle. "I walk through these alleys every three months," Sunni says. "By the end of October, it will be a year since this one site has been cleaned by the city." On a given day, the *Post-Dispatch* reported in July 2018, half of the city's eighty-four garbage trucks are out of service, having broken down, making sites like the one Sunni referenced common. The City of St. Louis is close to bankruptcy. With remaining services, like trash pickup, unevenly distributed, black neighborhoods are hit worse.

"We trying to get some fucking trash picked up here," Sunni says, laughing but not kidding.

Sunni and Shuron had connected over struggles dealing with their landlords in Gravois Park on the south side. Their time renting had often been fraught with issues of negligent ownership and upkeep.

Alongside residents of surrounding neighborhoods, they began organizing through the local community corporation, Dutchtown South. "We came together and started sharing stories about life on the south side." Residents were in the process of revamping Dutchtown's Community Empowerment Committee. "A topic kept coming up," Sunni explains, "the experience with poor quality housing and slumlords."

"I was waking up in the morning and having bed bug bites all over my body," Sunni says. "I was dealing with a swarm of rodents in my house." Without response from the property's owner, Sunni looked elsewhere for support. "I was calling the city to report it, but I was met with an unresponsive city government," she says, "so we went full force."

"To be honest, I hadn't heard of the 1969 rent strike," Sunni says. "Do you remember when we started talking about it?" she asks Shuron.

"We were going to the mall, I think," Shuron responds, "I was like, 'Yo, I just read this book, and the last chapter was dedicated to the rent strike. These women—these black women—did something that is almost unfathomable. They organized themselves. And they did it in this systematic way.'"

In the wake of the Great Depression, public housing was created for white families. Then, when the projects that were built became more integrated around the 1950s, white people began to leave. White families across income levels were given access to homeownership through federal loans at affordable rates created by the New Deal.

Black families, however, at the direction of the federal government, were locked out of the subsidized mortgage market. Between 1934 and 1968, 98 percent of federal home ownership loans went to whites, thereby constructing the nation's suburbs. Black people were all but confined to be renters, left with depleted city tax bases and failing services to match.

In the meantime, the values of suburban homes were further propped up by publicly subsidized highways, connecting city to suburb, through the Federal Highway Act of 1956—the largest public works project in the nation's history.

In addition to becoming racialized, public housing became gendered. New rules disqualified families with able-bodied men. Black women and children became the primary tenants of public housing.

In the midst of suburbanization, renters in the city fought for their homes. In 1967, sixty public housing tenants, primarily black women, picketed in front of the St. Louis Housing Authority. They called for rent reductions, pest control, and better clean up services. Historian Clarence Lang later argued, in *Grassroots at the Gateway*, that in doing so these women rejected male-oriented narratives assigning them a passive role in struggle, or one dependent on a male breadwinner.

Again in May of 1968, tenants took to the streets. 200 tenants marched to city hall, calling for rent reductions and reforms to Missouri's welfare system. They were backed this time by black power groups in St. Louis including the Black Liberators, the Zulu 1200's, and ACTION.

In November 1968, the St. Louis Housing Authority imposed yet another rent increase—despite HUD's disapproval. "We thought the rents were too high for the tenants to pay," said the director of housing at HUD to the *Post-Dispatch*. "We did not agree with the authority that the increase was the answer to its financial problems."

In response to the rent hike, organizers went door to door in the Carr Square and Vaughn buildings on the near north side of the city. By December 1968, over half the tenants living in those two buildings—approximately 800 families—committed to strike. Rent would be paid, instead of to the Housing Authority, into a joint account.

"This structure was planned," Shuron emphasises. "I don't wanna say they did it by the book, because they kind of wrote the book on it," she says in between sips. "They collectively organized to withhold all of their money in an escrow account."

"That history, these women, inspires us with tactics," Shuron says. "Of course we can get people affordable housing that is dignified and that someone actually wants to come home to—because these women did it, you know?"

As city leadership continued to ignore the group's demands, the coalition of tenants grew. The rent strike was to begin January 1, 1969.

On the south side, tenants in the Darst, Webbe, and Clinton-Peabody housing complexes came together, signing on to the rent strike. The south side coalesced around Jean King's leadership. Tenants elected King as chair of the Citywide Rent Strike Committee.

Over time, tenants of eight housing complexes across the city joined in. Each cluster operated their own tenant council. The Rev. Buck Jones, for example, led tenants at Carr Square and Vaughn, buildings which neighbored each other on the near north side. Jones had been a preacher since the age of fifteen and a community organizer for years before the strike.

Soon, well over a thousand public housing tenants were signed on to the strike—from the north side down to the south side. With numbers still growing, leadership, including King and Jones, pushed the start date back to ensure residents were organized. "For the first time," Jones said, "the people in public housing are consolidated into a power bloc that can get change."

On February 1 the strike began.

The late 1960s was a time of confrontation. The country was on the back end of the long civil rights movement. Malcolm X had been assassinated; so called "race riots," or uprisings, had literally burned through Newark, New Jersey, and Detroit, Michigan, in 1967; Stokely Carmichael, chairman of the Student Nonviolent Coordinating Committee, coined the term "black power"—defining it as "the coming together of black people to fight for their liberation by any means necessary." In doing so, he articulated the militancy in the air.

By that time, Dr. Martin Luther King Jr. had turned his attention to international and anti-capitalist struggles. Rev. King arrived in Memphis the spring of 1968 to support over 1,300 black sanitation workers on strike over working conditions and poverty wages.

"Something is happening in Memphis," Rev. King said on April 3, 1968. "Something is happening in our world." He was assassinated the following night.

A year after Rev. King's death, in St. Louis, the Rev. Buck Jones told the *Post-Dispatch*, "Now, more than ever before, I respect Dr. Martin Luther King Jr." Jones continued, "Judging from the number of people we have and dollars in the bank, we must have the right approach."

By the end of April 1969, those on strike had withheld over $140,000 in rent. Residents at Pruitt-Igoe had recently organized and joined the strike. Pruitt-Igoe consisted of thirty-three towers—each eleven stories high. In response, the Housing Authority filed eviction suits on seventy-three striking tenants and placed a lien on all overdue rents. By doing so, they effectively barred access to the collective accounts. "The Housing Authority closed the doors to the banks on us," Jones told the *Post-Dispatch*. "We are not throwing in the towel, though."

With the liens in place, organizers and their legal team collected and withheld rent outside of the banks. King, however, encouraged strike participants to spend their what-would-be rent money. As a result, many tenants moved out, renting private units or often even purchasing homes with saved up funds. Vacancy rates in the complexes spiked.

That May, King wrote to Mayor Cervantes:

> We feel that the poor people in your city should be congratulated for their fine behavior and nonviolent acts during this time you have taxed them to death in order that you might provide a happy and wealthy life for yourself and your henchmen. We wonder why you are playing a game with us. It is a very dangerous one you know. We didn't have to plead with you, and we won't plead any longer.

Sunni, considering her home, says, "These neighborhoods are just a part of a cycle."

Nationwide, black wealth and home ownership gains of the 1990s and early 2000s were attacked through the racialized predatory lending of subprime mortgages. In 2008 when the housing market crashed, half of all black wealth in the country was eliminated. The housing crisis hit Sunni's zip code, one that had a growing number of black homeowners, with particular force. "Black home ownership rates plummeted," she says, "Now the majority here, over 60 percent, are renters."

The neighborhoods where Sunni and Shuron focus their energies—Gravois Park, Dutchtown, Marine Villa, and Mount Pleasant—are just a few miles southwest of where Jean King called home.

The foreclosure crisis concentrated ownership. The prevalence of foreclosed properties in the neighborhoods created a ripe market for opportunistic buyers, many of whom stalled on investing in the units. Instead, the new landlords rented them out without improvement or held them vacant for years.

These neighborhoods, built up around the turn of the century, are full of brick buildings. Most are single family, with duplexes and four-units interspersed.

"Then cities add to the decline when they remove public services," Sunni says.

Today, the areas in the south side where Sunni and Shuron live and work are home to a high concentration of tenants receiving housing subsidies. Instead of next door to one another in high rises, families now live in a fractured landscape.

The iconic, nationally televised, 1972 demolition of the St. Louis housing project Pruitt-Igoe marked a shift, not just in the structural form, but also in the financial framework of low-income housing. The new program called Section 8 began in 1974 as a partnership between housing authorities and private rental markets. Tenants and their local housing authority would begin paying rent to private landlords. Under the oversight of local housing authorities, these landlords were responsible for the upkeep of their buildings.

Landlords outside of impoverished black communities have historically refused prospective tenants when presented with a voucher. Layers of disinvestment and denial of housing have concentrated both poverty and public housing tenants in places like Gravois Park in the city's twentieth ward. "The ward," Sunni says, "is over 78 percent people of color."

Since meeting, Sunni and Shuron have built community with residents, both those receiving subsidy and those not, across the south side.

"The first step was to just activate other people," Sunni says.

In the 1960s, tenants went next door or down the hall to talk with their neighbors about rent and unit conditions. Today, in neighborhoods where private ownership of publicly-subsidized rental units is high, conversations about housing and ownership happen in a different context. "We had to take this on the road," Sunni says of their organizing efforts.

Sunni recalls meetings with residents from across the neighborhoods, "It was so crazy when people started talking and sharing." She continues, "You had folks coming to meetings and finding out they had the same property owner or management company when they sat down and started voicing their grievances."

Shuron says, "Myisha and I even knew each other, but we didn't realize we had the same slumlord until we started talking at that meeting."

Sunni follows, "Yeah, and then Jara and I figured out we have the same slumlord, too."

The current fragmentation of public housing tenants limits collective bargaining power. The landscape positions individual tenants against landowners, who have the weight of rental law and access to wealth behind them. "There's no way some of these landlords should be getting a subsidy for these properties," Shuron says, "But they are. And they're getting it through the Housing Authority."

"At the moment our target is the slumlord, but one of our future targets has to be the Housing Authority. The St. Louis Housing Authority is allowing this mess to happen."

"What's also amazing," Sunni says, referring back to the rent strike, "is that they saw the intersectionality of their movement."

"Co-rrect!!" Shuron interjects.

The 1969 rent strike, while catalyzed by black women living in public housing, gained support from all over of the city. Harold Gibbons and his Teamsters Union provided financial support and assistance in negotiations with Mayor Cervantes and the Housing Authority. Black power collectives like the Zulu 1200's and the Black Liberators also provided organizational support.

ACTION, CORE, and the Black Arts Group (BAG), too, aided in dramatizing the conflict of the rent strike. BAG created music and theater as well as hosted weekly meetings for tenants at the building they owned on Washington Avenue.

The Legal Aid Society of St. Louis offered their skills. Lawyers continually fought off the city and the Housing Authority. They warded off eviction threats and kept tenants from losing their withheld rent money.

"That's one thing that's always brought up," Sunni says, "How does our movement intersect with other movements like black liberation, the struggle for LGBQIA+ rights, immigrant rights, labor, those fighting for a higher minimum wage?" She continues, "We understand that these are the same populations usually most affected by housing issues, too."

Community Empowerment Committee's recent mass meetings built a network of allies and members. Still, Sunni notes, "We are in the beginning of it. We know how crucial it is to connect with the people on the north side and in North County. They are us. They look like us. They, economically, are the same."

In July of 1969, with tensions high, HUD sent a private contractor to investigate St. Louis's public housing conflict. Edgar Ewing's report called the projects in St. Louis "the worst in nation."

The following week, King made a trip to Washington to testify in front of the Senate. She shared her case and that of St. Louis on the national stage with the support of Massachusetts senator Edward Brooke.

Back in St. Louis, things came to a head. The strike brought the St. Louis Housing Authority to the very brink of bankruptcy. By October, over 2,400 tenants from the eight public housing projects had withheld well over $600,000—today's equivalent of $4.5 million.

The Authority reported back to HUD that mass closure of public housing was inevitable if the strike continued. They made plans to shut down the complexes and evict the tenants in January 1970. Public housing residents were unphased; the strike persisted. Worn down, after nine months, Mayor Cervantes and the Housing Authority agreed to the tenants' demands. Rent would be based on a tenant's ability to pay. A tenants' affairs board was created to amplify residents' voices. Further, tenants were to be included on the St. Louis Housing Authority's Board of Commissioners.

King's recommendation, included in her testimony, that rent for publicly assisted housing be income-based, was included in the Brooke Amendment of the Housing Act of 1969. The amendment capped rent at 25 percent of a public housing tenant's income. As a result, federal subsidies increased nationwide to cover the differences.

Today, HUD's federal standard—that no more than 30 percent of a subsidized household's income should go to rent—is owed in large part to pressure created by St. Louis residents. Shortly after President Ronald Reagan was elected, he directed the 25 percent cap be raised to 30 percent.

"It touched everybody all over the country who lived in public housing," King later wrote, reminiscing on the strike. "I'm very proud of that."

Still, the win was not achieved without its toll. Jean King worked a full-time job—nights at Malcolm Bliss Hospital, from 11:00 p.m. to 7:00 a.m. During the day, she routinely spent nine hours on rent strike activities, two of which were focused on reading about social movements. As a parent, King depended on her mother for childcare while organizing tenants. In just the first two months of the strike, King fainted three times from exhaustion.

Following the strike, King built her career on reshaping low-income housing. King and Richard Baron, a lawyer whom King met just prior to the strike in 1968, formed McCormack Baron and Associates, a group dedicated to building quality low-income rental units. King ran some of Baron's first developments in Cleveland and continued working with him back in St. Louis as the business grew to be one of the most prominent of its kind.

Shuron says, "It's bananas how they would walk to all the housing projects—walk all the way downtown to city hall. I'm like, 'No thank you. I ain't walking to city hall. That ain't happenin'.' But they did it. I couldn't."

"She says that now," Sunni responds, "But she would. She would walk." She turns to Shuron, "Listen, we start at my house. . . . It's not bad."

"I guess I would," Shuron agrees.

Post-Apocalypse Walking Tour

EILEEN G'SELL

"This is, genuinely, my idea of beauty. This is life after cities. This is life after humans."

We are staring at fifty-seven acres of overgrown wildlife comprising the former Pruitt-Igoe, one of the most iconic modernist feats in the history of public housing, and also one of the most catastrophic failures.

The "we" in question is South African cultural producer and arts practitioner Stephen Hobbs and myself, a native St. Louisan, who has lived in enough places to appreciate the utter strangeness of my place of provenance. It's fall 2015. We are sitting in the vacant parking lot of the Rhema Baptist Church off of Cass Avenue, a contemporary edifice so cleanly banal that, in this context, it feels spectacular.

I've been to the Pruitt-Igoe site before, in the spring, with an academic group investigating the fettered history of the city's development and decline in light of the shockwaves following the unrest in Ferguson. In 2011, I attended a screening of the documentary *The Pruitt-Igoe Myth* at a packed church off North Grand. I'd thought, before seeing it for real, that I'd know what to expect. But I did not, of course, know what to expect. How could I? How, truly, could anyone, given its eerie scale of emptiness and neglect?

Stepping over the "Keep Out" chain with Hobbs this sunny October afternoon, my sense of emptiness shifts. Teeming with insects, bushes, weeds, and brush, the rustle of leaves flirting with fall, the grave of Pruitt-Igoe is one of simultaneous blankness and fecundity. It is blank insofar as it is devoid of human presence; indeed, aside from a few sidewalk pedestrians off of Cass granting polite, if quizzical, glances our direction, nobody's around. But its verdant quality swings to life as Hobbs avidly snaps a series of shots. "A Google Earth image of Pruitt-Igoe would be amazing, I would think," he says.

Pruitt-Igoe was built around 1954, the year my father was born, at the height of white flight into the St. Louis suburbs and following the erasure of DeSoto-Carr, the historic African American neighborhood at the west edge of downtown. I say "erasure" because, after years of driving past the former Desoto-Carr from Grand Center to downtown, I'd had no idea that the area was once one of the most densely populated spots in town. I'd had no idea, in fact, that there had been a community there at all, but puzzled over the lack of architectural, residential, and commercial presence that characterized the contiguous neighborhoods.

At first, I'm admittedly wondering if all of this is old hat to Hobbs—after all, he has just been to Detroit, to Cleveland; St. Louis is his last stop on the rust belt circuit, and he's been here but two days. I'm also wondering how his decades interrogating the incredible vibrancy—and violence—of Pan-African Johannesburg, *his* place of provenance, affects his perspective of a city also, if quite differently, fraught by a maze of contradictions and injustice.

"Just like Detroit and just like Cleveland, St. Louis, as part of the rust belt, exhibits the height of a particular industrial endeavor and its accompanying dismantling and collapse," says Hobbs. We are at the corner of Jefferson and Cass, examining two new bright billboards adjacent to two dilapidated brick buildings. One billboard features an image of an ebullient black woman lifting weights, ostensibly to fend of cancer; the other depicts a beaming nuclear family of color. Who is it, I think, that they smile at? They seem to be smiling at each other.

I ask Hobbs how this area compares to Johannesburg, and he responds, "I think it's safe to say that South Africa is about 90 percent more violent than where we are right now." What should alarm instead proves a somewhat refreshing statement from someone with what initially sounds like a posh, European accent, so accustomed am I to the outsider conclusion that I live in a dangerous place, that the city I was born in is scary, more threatening than anywhere else.

The man who designed Pruitt-Igoe, a Japanese architect named Minoru Yamasaki, also designed the main terminal of the Lambert International Airport, as well as the late World Trade Center. I say "late" because it occurs to me that any building that lives, that really lives, and then dies, entirely dies, deserves that kind of modifier. Do not buildings have a type of soul—one borne of the numberless human souls that at one time clanged or chimed inside?

If that is the case, then it is no surprise that Pruitt-Igoe is haunted. From 1954 to 1972, some thirty-three buildings of eleven stories each inhabited the territory; within its first decade, they were almost exclusively filled with African American families. In total nearly three thousand units were stacked toward the sky, in which, across the years, tens of thousands lived, laughed, and suffered, and from which tens of thousands left. The site was cleared by 1976, three years before I was born, and three years after Hobbs was, some 8,797 miles, or 14,157 kilometers, away.

I am surprised at first that Stephen Hobbs hadn't known of Pruitt-Igoe, but then, of course, why would he? I hadn't heard of it till my late twenties, and I spent a large part of my childhood and schooling in St. Louis. My father is from North County. My mother went to St. Louis University, a mere line drive away from the former Desoto-Carr. The most obvious explanation for my ignorance is that I am white, and that, as a white person, my experience of St. Louis—its realities, its legends, its tragic legacies—have long been filtered through a lens of power. How many black voices have gone missing in the process?

"The abandoned modernist project is, at the end of the day, just natural earth," says Hobbs as we pull out of the Rhema lot. "The earth will just push right through it. It's its own life cycle. That's what I'm currently investigating—the presence of absence, what could be, the myths that are hiding in that forest."

If there is beauty here now, it is surely elegiac.

A version of "Post-Apocalypse Walking Tour" was originally published in October 2018 in the Common Reader, Washington University in St. Louis's *"Journal of the Essay."*

Midnight Annie's Final Performance

CHRIS ANDOE

I woke up on Wednesday, September 24, 2014, grabbed my phone from the nightstand, and checked social media like I always did. The first post I saw was from a friend announcing that the bar where I spent my Friday nights, Clementine's, was closing after the coming weekend. I was floored, and hoped it was just a rumor. The historic corner bar and restaurant, famous for their strong drinks and colorful characters, was one of my favorite things about St. Louis. It was the LGBT community's embassy in Soulard, and for me symbolized permanence.

Entombed in the wall of the establishment were the remains of Midnight Annie, a drag queen who long frequented and performed at the bar. While laughing and drinking there with my friend Big David, I sometimes pondered having my own remains interred beside her, forever being part of the action. She passed in April 1995 at the age of seventy-three, two years before I first moved to St. Louis, but I felt like I knew her after hearing so many tales of her antics. Her shows sounded like pure madness. She'd often sit down on stage, wearing her salt and pepper bouffant wig and sequin gown, and begin kicking up her heels and howling at the moon.

All morning I tried to get confirmation as I began working on the article. Bars were always rumored to be closing, and there'd been embarrassing retractions in the past. One bar, Novak's, even had an emotional closing gala, only to open up for business as usual the following day. The LGBT magazine I wrote for, *Vital Voice*, had to balance the desire to break the story with the need to get it right, and our publisher decided we weren't running the piece until we had a quote from one of the owners.

Rather than covering it as breaking news, I crafted the announcement like a eulogy, recalling the storied past of the place, how it was a cornerstone of the community, was the oldest surviving LGBT bar in St. Louis, and how there was no more prestigious spot to be during Mardi Gras than on the grand balcony above the entrance. In 2012, I was so determined to grace that balcony that I loitered around the guarded entrance to the upper floor, and the second the bouncer's back was turned, bolted up the stairs. I strolled in like I was supposed to be there, tossing beads into the crowd below for ten or fifteen minutes until I sensed suspicion from the krewe, and nonchalantly made my exit.

The article was essentially written when I arrived at Clem's and spoke to the bartender, who'd just learned the news himself in a letter from owner Gary Reed. It was then I got word that #Boom, Vital Voice's bitter rival, had just broken the story with a brief announcement and a quote from the same bartender. We ran our piece twenty minutes later. I then began working on gathering and documenting every story I could from the patrons during the remaining days. I knew my Friday night group, but there were so many people I didn't know. People who were there during the day, or on different nights. I needed to meet and talk to as many of them as I could in a desperate attempt to immortalize this place before it was too late. With a pen in one hand and a cocktail in the other, I lived, breathed, and drank the moment. During those final days, I was embedded at Clem's.

"It's like Cheers, when I'm down and out there's always someone here to lift me up. That's the one thing that scares me to death: Where am I going to meet my friends? Where will us fading flowers go?" said Josie, a heavyset man of fifty-two.

That first night the news was so fresh and most everyone was in disbelief while some were angry. A festive, slender man of about sixty, named Johnnie, was excited about my interviews, and told me who I should speak with.

"See the guy with the hot pink goblet? That's Miss Davey. He's been coming here every single day for years and they keep that goblet just for him. One day I asked Jan, 'How do I get my own goblet?' and she said, 'Well, you've gotta come here every day!' You need to talk to him!" Johnny said, but returned a moment later, "He's too upset and is afraid of what he might say. Give him a little time."

I spoke to a big, gruff, bearded man named Dennis who, in his booming voice, told me Clem's was his first gay bar, then a frail, petite man walked through the door and Dennis shouted, "HEY HOWARD!" and pulled him in. "This is Howard, he was here for the grand opening!"

I greeted Howard, who told me he was seventy-nine and lived on the east side. "I always stopped here to get my bridge drink," he said. I suggested he grab a cocktail and then come back to talk.

"You're giving him too much time, he might die in the next five minutes! He's about a hundred and forty!" Dennis joked.

Later, at the tables on the old brick sidewalk out front, Dennis and his buddies agreed to tell me more stories if I'd smoke a joint with them.

A group of six men shared tales about Clem's, reminisced about other bars that came and went over the years, and recalled the tales of Midnight Annie. Legend had it she got the name back in the 1940s when she'd bribe a jailer to let her "entertain" inmates in the middle of the night.

"Oh I remember Midnight Annie," one man began. "She was a trust fund baby and when she'd get an installment, she'd blow it in no time. Once she sauntered into a Cadillac dealership and bought *two* Cadillacs. One for her and one for her trick! That's just how she was. God, I still remember her sitting at that bar drunk as hell with her lipstick going up her wrinkled face and her wig on crooked. She had this trademark high-pitched sound she'd make, and when she'd do it everyone around the bar would mimic it. Like a bird call."

Many of the stories about St. Louis's gay world came out of East St. Louis because gay bars were less likely to be raided there. Some of the bars sounded a lot like speakeasies.

"Those early days were revolutionary," began a silver-haired gentleman named Beaux. "There were bars that were straight by day and gay by night, and Helen Schrader's started out that way. Helen had been a notorious madam with fifty women working for her during her heyday. When one of her first girls, Alice, got old, she worked the front door at the bar. You'd knock and Miss Alice would slide a little slot open and look at you. If she knew you, she'd let you in. If she didn't, she'd tell you to go away."

Stories also came in online. My friend Dan posted a memory on Facebook, and it really struck me because it was about a passing generation:

One really busy night many years ago I had sex right there on the counter of the bar, maybe 400 in the bar at the time. Surprised? It brought back memories of the first owner, Wally Thomas. He sold it in '85 but it stayed a gay bar. People don't want to let go, but the past HAS to go. The past, the bars, the buildings, the people all have had their time and now need to go. And they will—no matter what is said. That place leaves far greater a legacy than I ever will. As one person said: The old heart of Gay St. Louis will cease to beat. I see the passages. The old gay ghettos, the book stores, the peep shows, the gay bars, their time has passed. My tribe, my people, my places, become part of yesterday's mist. Museum pieces that fade and collect dust. And so does yours truly.

While Monday would be the last day, Sunday afternoon was when the community at large came to say their goodbyes. It looked like Mardi Gras as the crowd spilled out of the bar into the street, where a BMW blasted music for the hundreds of people outside.

I had only been back in town for a few months, having moved to San Francisco to try to salvage a long beleaguered relationship, and then to New York to get over it. My heart, however, was always in St. Louis, and I was so thankful to be on the ground during these final days of Clementine's. It would have killed me to miss them.

Steve Potter, a local NPR personality, was so moved and inspired by the stories Clem's fading flowers shared with *Vital Voice* that he came out on the air, discussing his first visit to the bar decades earlier.

As the world opened up, gay bars nationwide were going the way of the dinosaur, especially those serving an older clientele. But this haunted town had such a memory, and rather than disappear, Clem's would simply take its place in the local folklore.

I almost didn't go to closing night, and Big David didn't plan on going either. It was a Monday, I'd spent every waking hour there since Wednesday, and I thought it would be too sad. Around eight, however, I decided I would always regret not going. Since I was going, Big David came out as well. I walked in, and on the glowing dry erase marquee near the pool table I wrote, "Going down with the ship."

The bar was crowded but not overly so, and the characters there were the ones who really loved the place. The spirits were higher than expected and the camaraderie was simply incredible as old friends hugged, laughed, and made toasts. Miss Davey, the daily regular who had his own hot pink goblet and had been too upset to be interviewed, came up and gave me a hug.

"I'm really sad, but I'm going to be okay," he said, smiling.

When owner Gary and his late partner Jim bought the bar in 1985, they held their first drag show. Midnight Annie was the headliner. Unbeknownst to her, they promoted the evening as "Midnight Annie's Final Performance" to make it more of a draw.

"Would you quit telling people this is my final performance?" an exasperated Midnight Annie kept admonishing.

I was less than a foot from Gary when, in the final hours, he took the mic, and the quiet, introverted man who'd hardly said anything over the years gave a rousing farewell speech. The whole place stopped to listen. He spoke about how much times had changed since the bar opened in 1978, and changed for the better. He spoke of the historic old brick building which was erected in the 1860s. He said all drinks were on the house until the last bottle was dry, and then he brought up Midnight Annie.

"I always say my only child was a seventy-three year old drag queen," he began, "and she's leaving with me. Ladies and Gentleman, next to Jan is Midnight Annie!"

I'll be goddamned if he didn't have Midnight Annie's dusty urn—complete with the yellowed and water-stained label—sitting there on the bar with a cocktail.

The crowd erupted with cheers and applause.

On that final evening there were people in attendance who'd come to see Midnight Annie's final performance back in 1985. After a thirty year wait, she and Gary Reed finally delivered with a closing number the city will never forget.

Midnight Annie, courtesy of Kage Black

A version of "Midnight Annie's Final Performance" was first published in Vital Voice.

MEMORIES

The Moments That Shaped Us

Sunup to Sundown

VIVIAN GIBSON

Many of the women on Bernard Street, including my grandmother, left home before daylight to catch as many as three streetcars that transported them to manicured communities just west of the city limits. They arrived early to homes where they cooked and served scrambled eggs for breakfast, and readied white children for school. The rest of their day was spent cooking, cleaning, and doing laundry until boarding streetcars in the evening that returned them home just in time to go to bed. Grandmama said that there were "sundown laws" that mandated people of color to be off the streets in St. Louis County by sunset. If she had to work late, her "white folks" (that's how she referred to her employers) would drive her to the Wellston Loop to catch an eastbound streetcar back into the city.

My grandmother was in bed for the night by 7:30, which was our time to be quiet. An often slammed front door, a burst of laughter, or the rhythmic thumps of Sam Cooke singing "Another Saturday night and I ain't got nobody" on the radio, would elicit familiar rapping on her bedroom floor. There was a broomstick leaning against the wall—an arm's length away, just for the purpose of pounding a signal for silence. Sometimes, out of frustration, she would shuffle in her well-worn bedroom slippers to the top of the stairs and call down in a commanding tone, made no less threatening by her shaky, weary voice: "Frances, make those children be quiet." It usually worked for the rest of the evening.

My favorite retreat from the constant hum made by the remaining nine people inhabiting the three small rooms below was halfway up the stairs that led to Grandmama's rooms on the second floor. The worn wooden risers and treads of the steps created a perfect work desk for cutting out Betsy McCall paper dolls. The eagerly anticipated monthly issue of *McCall's Magazine* provided me with hours of cutting out brightly colored paper dresses, coats, and hats that I carefully crimped onto Betsy's posed body. More hours were spent drawing new outfits of my own design. Using the smooth white cardboard that formed Daddy's freshly laundered Sunday shirts into starched folded rectangles, I cut and crafted small easels that held my paper dolls erect for my private fashion shows.

That space that divided Grandmama's quietness from our perpetual hum held another appeal for me—it was my opportunity to eavesdrop on my grandmother's cloistered existence just feet away. There was always a low murmur from her brown molded plastic Zenith radio that sat on the crowded table just inside her bedroom door. The black rotary telephone that took up most of the remaining space on the small table rarely rang in the evening. But when it did ring, I leaned in and pressed the side of my face against the wooden upright balusters and positioned an ear to hear what was said. Sometimes I could tell it was one of the mothers from the church, usually Mother Vine. Mother Vine was a feisty and friendly old lady who always smiled and stroked my face on Sunday mornings when we arrived at the church. She tilted my chin upward and looked me in my eyes in a way that my grandmother never did. She would always ask "How's yo' mama?" as if to distract me while she magically presented a peppermint candy from her purse. I couldn't see Grandmama's face, but I could hear a slight smile in her voice after she said, "Hey Vine" into the phone receiver. Their phone conversations never lasted long and ended with a wry, knowing chuckle followed by, "you get some rest now, bye."

Other times when the phone rang I would hear a voice and words that I hardly recognized. Grandmama's side of the phone conversation started with the usual questioning "hello?" Then it changed to an unfamiliar subservient "yes ma'am." After a pause her voice changed again to a soothing maternal tone that I only heard during these exchanges, "I know," she'd say reassuringly, "you be a good boy now. Go to bed, and I'll be there when you wake up in the morning."

Restorative Faith

CHRISTOPHER ALEX CHABLÉ

This time, the miracle was a tortilla burn
revealing the Bird Man of Cahokia.
I called Francis from this catholic city
and said, "Jorge, I forgot the poem
where Avila pierces her heart with Cupid's arrow
and cums on the stump of the tree of Jesse."
"You never get to see the virgin anymore, *Compa.*
Call her sometime." Our feet are always
in the water, Bird Man's and mine. Shallow
is the bank of the Mississippi where the vagabond
tent settles behind us. He won't talk. We cut the rinds
from the avocados and let the current sail them.

Kenny

JOAN NIESEN

Kenny was there in the sixties, my mom always said, back when Conway Road was a bunch of farms and her friend, Betsy from City House, lived all the way out there in the boonies. My mom would go play at Betsy's house, where there were cats, and Kenny was the man who owned the property next door, about a mile west of what's now Mercy Hospital.

My mom was a U. City kid, and my dad grew up in St. Louis Hills before moving to Ladue as a teenager. They were city people, disdainful of the suburbs, but when my dad got a job as a surgeon at St. Luke's Hospital in Chesterfield, living east of Lindbergh wasn't an option. "West of Lindbergh," my mom always said, spitting the phrase out like a swear word. "I can't believe I live west of Lindbergh."

In 1987, my parents built a house on a cul-de-sac off of Conway Road, about one hundred yards from Kenny's plot of land. I was six months old when we moved in, and our little family watched without really noticing as the duck pond next door became a subdivision, as old ranches were demolished to make way for West County mansions. By the mid-nineties, as St. Louis pushed farther and farther west, our too-far-out home became something like centrally located. By then, farmland didn't start for another twenty miles, and Conway Road bore the traffic of several schools and dozens of subdivisions. It was unrecognizable from my mom's first trip—except for Kenny, who sat on so much property his house was barely visible from the street. He had a gravel driveway that led back down across his sloping lawn, and nearly every day, Kenny sat at the top of it, about a foot from the curb: retired, shirtless, and perpetually sunburned, perched on his John Deere and waving.

Kenny was our Conway Road eccentric. I couldn't tell you how I knew his name, or when I learned it, but it's what we called him, my brother and I and the carpool of boys my mom drove from MICDS down Conway Road almost every afternoon. It's how I introduced him to my friends when we drove by—"introduced" in the sense that I'd wave and laugh and explain that he wasn't just some old man, he was Kenny. Someone knew someone who'd told us his name, just like someone once told my mom that Kenny ate dinner every night at the Frontenac Hilton. I always wondered if that was true, until one day he pulled out of his lane in front of me and drove his big white cruise ship of a car east down Conway to Lindbergh to the Hilton. I followed him, just to be sure.

There's no sidewalk on the north side of Conway, where Kenny always sat, which added to the mystery. You could never, without trying at least, really get close enough to talk. I could have crossed, I suppose, a thousand or so times, and asked how he was doing—or what his name was, or how the mowing had gone. But his name was Kenny, I was sure, and I never actually saw him mow, and he always seemed to be doing fine, smiling and waving and basking in the swampy St. Louis summer. The man was a part of the landscape as much as the giant pine tree he always parked in front of, tanned and creased and a little bit shiny. I always thought he looked a little bit like a thinner Billiken, a human good luck charm of the summertime suburbs.

In the eighties, my mom pushed me past Kenny in my stroller. In the nineties, when I'd run away from home—upset and crying for reasons so trivial as being told to read the flier I was given at Sunday School—I still stopped to wave at Kenny on my angry trudge east, and again five minutes later on my resigned walk home. In the throes of a short-lived eating disorder in my early teens, I wandered past Kenny and wondered what was happening to my brain and my body, a pound or two thinner every time I passed him, and eventually a pound or two healthier again. At fifteen, I drove my dad's mortifying car—a silver Ford Taurus—down Conway Road without a driver's license when I knew I wouldn't get caught, going too fast with all the windows down and the Cardinals broadcast cranked on KMOX. I slowed for Kenny, and sometimes I tooted my horn, which would get an extra-long wave—just like I would every time I drove my Honda Civic to and from school, or my lifeguarding job, or wherever I was going too fast and with too much on my mind once I was sixteen and free. I told my friends, and my boyfriends, to roll down their windows. When I went to the East Coast for college and was horribly homesick, Kenny's first wave over fall break sent me into tears.

I've lived away from St. Louis since 2006, but my parents still have the same house and I visit close to a dozen times a year. For a long time, Conway Road was a comfort. As volatile as my twenties were—moves across the country for jobs in journalism, bad relationships, worse paychecks—the street stayed the same, frozen as I'd left it, and more beautiful once I stopped taking it for granted. Maybe a tree limb would fall one year, and a house would get repainted the next, and someone would get a new dog. Kenny was still there, still old, still wrinkled, still sunburned—but no older or more weathered than he'd ever been it seemed. He was a constant among constants, which is why, even after I became a writer, a professional information-seeker, I never looked into his story. I never crossed to the north side of the street, never stopped my car along the curb and introduced myself and asked him to do the same. I didn't want to see Kenny through the eyes of an adult, a journalist, a skeptic.

Kenny died a few years ago, in 2014. My mom told me she thought it was coming. He was out less on the John Deere, and when he was there, the man who hadn't seemed to age in fifty years finally looked decrepit. He waved slower, nodded less, and then one day he simply wasn't there. A "For Sale" sign popped up on the property, which a developer snapped up. The neighborhood they built where Kenny's house used to be is almost finished. The four behemoth houses are that special brand of ornate ugly that exists in white-collar suburbs where people aren't sure if they want to build themselves a French chateau or an English manor and settle on some mash-up of the two. It's called Windsor Oaks now. They cut down the giant pine.

When I drive by, I wave at Kenny's ghost. I wonder why he spent so many years of his life waving back at me—and I don't need to know the answer.

Playbill

JOHN HICKS

Silent
in the winter cold,
they shrug and back away
from the playbill at the Powell,
tacked up for tonight.

She, pinched waist.
He, stiffly stoic
A cello and an oboe—
players encased
in battered black.
Their gig cancelled
by the light-bulbed
marquee that trumpets
a staccato groove:
   Held Over One Night

They drift into shadow,
going wherever musicians go
when their gig is trumped
by another.

Moon of the Disappearing Water

DEBORAH JACKSON TAFFA

We were living at the far western edge of St. Louis, within walking distance of a twenty-acre lake that disappeared overnight. Millions of gallons of water vanished, and by mid-morning all that was left was a brown pool over a sinkhole, as if a giant had pulled the plug at the deep end of a bathtub and the water was still making its way down the drain. Dying fish, mostly big bass, flopped around on the muddy ground trying to stay wet. Herons and vultures fed on them, pecking their bodies apart, gorging themselves on the unexpected windfall. The fish that had managed to escape the birds' feast lay gasping for oxygen, their gills working desperately. A rancid odor wafted toward the highway across an open field, away from the residential neighborhoods that made up the southern, western, and eastern shores.

The disappearance of Lake Chesterfield made the national news and throngs of people came to gawk at the sight. Suddenly we had news vans stationed at the entrance to our subdivision. The city sent cops, who reserved a section of curb with orange cones for the television crews and then stood in the street directing traffic. Reporters jockeyed for vantage points in order to tape their segments. Satellites, mounted atop media vans, uplinked images. A slew of SUVs and minivans arrived to bottleneck the street. Our neighbors complained about blocked driveways. They left angry notes under windshield wipers and said the cops weren't ticketing fast enough.

I stood in the living room and watched as our subdivision flashed across the television. There was the club house with the phony Cape Cod façade, the tennis courts with neat plastic turf, the lighthouse in miniature, the adult-only pool and the family pool. Seeing the television images of dank earth and the beaks ripping fish flesh, my stomach soured. My husband, Simone, and I had recently discovered we were expecting another child. We were struggling to make ends meet, fighting about childcare and whether or not St. Louis would become our permanent home.

Our neighbor, Mr. Emmett, a forest ranger, came to the door. "You've got to see it with your own eyes," he said.

I went upstairs and told the kids to put their shoes on.

My children and I had been in the habit of exploring the lake's wooded side on foot. Several times a week, we would walk over to skip stones and sip honeysuckle from a bush that grew just beyond a small inlet with an arching bridge. They liked to play "Billy Goats Gruff" and always fought over who got to run ahead, go down to the shore, and assume the troll's role. They settled the argument by recruiting me. Then I would hurry into position—deepen my voice to yell the lines, "Trip-trap, trip-trap! Who dares to cross over my bridge?"—and grab at their ankles through the slats as they passed screaming.

When it was hot and muggy, as it often is in St. Louis, the thick canopy on the wooded side provided shade. We traveled up and back on the same shore rather than circling the lake for this reason, but also because retracing our steps allowed us to avoid traffic on the far side. The road into our neighborhood passed on one side of the lake alone; the honeysuckle trail was abutted by woods, the backsides of homes obscured by trees. We took our time on these walks. Most days, we had the trail to ourselves.

Now the human activity around the lake had exponentially grown and our familiar routine felt invaded. We left our house and walked quickly. My oldest daughter, Miquela, paused at the trailhead, curious about the cop directing traffic at the corner, but I held on to the hands of my younger two kids and kept moving. When we passed the bridge and the little faux lighthouse came into view, Miquela was still straggling behind and I called for her to hurry. Reeds and other plants were exposed where emerald green water used to be. Carrion appeared as we neared the lake's drain. From the muddy shore I could see the brown pool ahead. The bulk of people, locals and visitors, had congregated nearest the sinkhole, across from each other on either side of the lake's thinnest section.

We arrived at the edge of the crowd. I dropped my two little kids' hands and stopped. I could see an ancient shopping cart at the center of the lake bed. It was tipped on its side and had algae strung over it like tinsel. The bones of a large, picked-apart fish jutted up in the air near one of its wheels.

I squeezed by a cyclist to get closer. Sidling up, I heard a group of mothers talking. "It doesn't smell as bad as I thought," one of them said.

Another pointed north, saying, "It does on that side of the lake—better pray the wind doesn't change."

They grimaced. Their kids blew bubbles with chewing gum and turned cartwheels in the grass. The mothers told them not to wander off, then turned to coo over a chubby newborn. Taking in the party-like atmosphere, I considered the capacity a little carnage has to attract a crowd.

We overheard conversations about how much the disaster was going to cost the homeowner's association. Wanting to ask questions, I looked for neighbors. But we'd only been living in St. Louis for two years and I didn't recognize anyone. I saw an athletic woman with long black hair and thought of Toke, my only Navajo friend in the Midwest. She had moved back to New Mexico almost as soon as she'd moved in.

Suddenly my daughter, Sonora, pulled at my arm and wanted to know why the water disappeared. She thought the earth was solid. Most importantly, what happened to the turtles? When I told her I didn't know what happened to the turtles she spoke quietly.

"We liked the turtles," she said.

I listened for more but that was it. We liked the turtles. She reminded me of the turtles' gracefulness in the water. In an instant I could see the greenish gray of their shells as they sunbathed on the rocks. I remembered the way they turned their noses up snottily when we came too close, plunging into the depths and gliding out of sight.

Soon her little brother chimed in. "Sonora's right," he said. "I don't see them anywhere."

Miquela found us in the crowd. She said she overheard speculation about an underground cavern. She stood with her mouth hanging open, looking over the surreal absence of water, our picturesque trail and perfect suburban life exposed. A noisy crow swooped down and started pecking at a still-living fish. The wind shifted. A rancid odor hit. The women near me plugged their noses and gathered their kids.

The smell made my eyes water. Sonora started sniffling about the turtles; her little brother flopped down on the grass, disturbed by her tears.

Miquela was outraged. "What about the fish? Some of them are still sucking for air!"

I thought of our neighbor, Mr. Emmett. I wished we knew him well enough to drop in for a glass of lemonade and some grandfatherly reassurance. I wanted someone to bolster the kids and explain the tenuous ground, the suffocating fish, the disappeared turtles. Of course, the people I really wanted were in Arizona. Mr. Emmett could never replace my father and uncles back home on the rez.

I missed the Southwest. I missed grilling quail with Dad in back of my Uncle Mick's house on the Yuma Reservation where we had lived before moving to St. Louis. I missed having him to our house. We lived farther out on the reservation than Mick, where you didn't have to deal with lights from the casino. We lived in the new sub, where every third house had real curtains. These were our responsible neighbors, mostly elderly women. They had chain link fences and grass. Our yard was dirt because all our earnings were spent on the kids. But after it grew dark we moved our lawn chairs out from the carport and could see every star in the sky.

The loneliness of the suburbs—"the leprosy of the West," as Mother Theresa called it—was sapping my certainty. In the absence of relatives, parenting is a huge responsibility. I'd become the sole portal for history, the only teacher of traditions for my kids. In a neighborhood built on notions of upward mobility, we were isolated, living among strangers. Such isolation creates the same complications for all families, regardless of their cultural origins: the loss of the ability to be a posterity.

Sonora pulled her shirt up over her nose. Her little brother rolled onto his stomach and buried his face. I didn't know how to console them. Reservation schools suck. Being poor sucks. When my truck-driving brother started a crating company in Albuquerque, we were happy to join him. When the movers we did business with offered us a St. Louis location, we lost the coin toss and moved to the Midwest. I don't know when this career sacrifice had begun to feel like a mistake. Could moneymaking justify robbing our children of family traditions and interactions with their elders?

Sonora grew angry. "You mean we're just going to let all these fish be eaten alive?"

Mr. Emmett hadn't mentioned the dying fish. Like everyone, he was concerned about fixing the lake for real estate values. Simone would argue that this viewpoint was valid and I knew he was right. I wouldn't want to flip upside-down in our mortgage. Neither would I let my four-year-old wander while I waded out with a net on a rescue mission.

The kids continued to badger me. "What are you going to do?"

As the crowd scattered, I watched every face, thinking someone might be moved by the dying fish and make a plan. If someone took the lead, I'd follow. I'd volunteer if someone watched the kids. I glanced at a large bass near the sinkhole, its gills sucking for oxygen, and began counting how many were still alive. What would my parents say about so much flesh left to waste? Would my neighbors think I was nuts if I knocked on doors and suggested bass for dinner?

I imagined my elders out there in the mud, the bird clan singing songs, someone burning sage for the fish. It was an incongruent image. I said, "Back home the fish wouldn't be wasted."

Sonora jumped to her feet. "I'm giving them a funeral."

Her certainty surprised me. On the reservation, grandparents led the way in prayer. Earning status as a traditionalist took years and, confirmed traveler that I was, I'd never taken on the responsibility. It was uppity to perform anything but private prayer duty, and watching my daughter act, I lamented my lack of confidence. For years I'd gotten by on the notion of staying quiet. I attended tribal ceremonies as a respectful participant, and once I became a foreigner, I visited home the way I traveled: I thought of myself as an outsider. It seemed grotesque to barge in on and tell locals how to live.

The last of our neighbors left without saying a word. Two teenagers hopped on their skateboards and rolled away. Soon everyone would be behind doors, locked inside air-conditioned cars, hidden behind sturdy brick homes that looked just like mine.

"I can't believe this crap," I said. "Back home there'd be people arriving in trucks with barbecue grills so that the fish wouldn't die for nothing."

My kids were holding hands with their heads together in prayer. I was happy they ignored my contempt. I took a deep breath. The smell was still terrible but my body had grown familiar and it was bearable.

I looked at the kids and reminded myself of the lectures I'd given them prior to every trip, every relocation. Our family travel philosophy: "No one's as foreign as they seem; every community has something to teach." If I really wasn't suburban material, why had we chosen to live here? Worse than my confusion was the greater instability: the ground had fallen away at our feet.

We had been in St. Louis for three years. After a decade of moving, we finally had a stable living arrangement. Four-star schools for our children felt like a miracle. Simone built his crates for high value antiques, artwork, baby grand pianos, grandfather clocks, and other breakable items. We got by.

"St. Louis?" my family raised their eyebrows when they learned we'd accepted the job. The majority of them couldn't conceive of leaving the Southwest.

Researching St. Louis, I saw that it ranked as one of the most segregated cities in America. Simone and I discussed the downside of leaving our West Coast lifestyle for the stolid Midwest, but we never seriously considered turning down the opportunity. Our main debate before moving involved where we should live in St. Louis. I argued for a suburb near Washington University with its libraries, art museums, coffee shops, and diversity. Simone balked. He hated urban areas with too much traffic.

Now, surrounded by wives who updated their décor every holiday season, I was dying for intellectual exchange and a community outside Holy Infant's soccer league and the kids' public elementary school. I missed like-minded people and serious conversations, yet I was also uncomfortable when neighborhood talks turned to politics. The well-traveled people I did find in our neighborhood worked for Monsanto. Dick Cheney and the Archbishop of St. Louis were regularly praised.

"It wouldn't be like this if we had bought a house in University City," I said.

"You never fit in anywhere, not even the reservation," Simone said, and then reminded me that the women in our neighborhood had been kind enough to throw me my first baby shower.

He shamed me into remembering that St. Louis was filled with kind people. The women from Holy Infant brought meals to sick neighbors and invited me to retreats. They silenced me when I complained. When I shared the fact that Simone didn't want me to return to school for a fine arts degree, they thought it was entirely reasonable. Why would I want to waste money on academic pursuits when there was little return on the investment?

Simone had grown up in Milano, in a skyscraper with only a small concrete patio for play. There had been a garden downstairs but the custodian stopped anyone who dared step foot on its grass. Simone claimed he was scarred by the experience. He professed a need for open space. I relented and we ended up in rural West County.

I wanted to make it work. I joined neighborhood coffees and book clubs. I volunteered at the elementary school. I taught two yoga classes at the YMCA and drew on my Laguna grandmother's Catholicism in discussions with my conservative Christian neighbors. When I helped at the food pantry and overheard two women from our parish complaining that their neighborhood had black families moving in, I told Simone they had to be the exception. Overhearing several neighbors, employees of Monsanto, arguing that climate change was a hoax, I bit my tongue.

"Ugh," my daughter said. "Is this smell ever going to go away?"

The final pool of water didn't seem to be receding. The drain looked clogged. If the last bit of lake water had diminished since we arrived, it was happening too slowly to see. Yet I knew the change was real and the next day the final drops would be gone and the last breathing fish would be dead. I felt a rush of nausea. My daughter was right. It felt as if the smell would never go away.

I took one last glance before leaving, imagining the lake flowing down into an unseen cavern, water sucked away by a sudden current no one had predicted, a waterfall plunging fish and turtles into cold darkness. I stared at the fish parked in the mud at the edge of the drain. The ones that had looked over the edge yet trickled to a halt just before taking the plunge. Lucky or unlucky, I wondered. Better to die slowly or quickly?

The flopping fish were the lucky ones. They at least got to die in the sun. I imagined those who went down the drain, their last glimpse of the horizon, the stars and moon above them as they took the plunge. I imagined their efforts to escape, swimming away from the giant inhalation, twisting as they went over the edge. If their fall was lucky, their brains were smashed by rocks. Otherwise they would freeze to death in complete and foreign darkness.

"Maybe we can call the Humane Society," I told the kids, knowing it would be futile.

It was time to leave the lake, to escape the sight and smell.

"Let's get out of here," I said. We ran at a slow pace so that the smaller two kids could keep up and when we rounded the bend and crossed the bridge no one stopped to look down for an imaginary ogre. From there, the lake bed was particularly ugly in its visibility; the fading light reflected off bottles, grocery bags, and other debris. We averted our eyes. As we neared the trailhead the smell diminished and we slowed to a walk.

The kids brooded on the familiar sidewalk home. I told them the lake's disappearance was a perfect example of the earth's unpredictable nature. "The earth always has the upper hand," I said, "no matter how much we want to control it." I told them that our lives were governed by chance, perhaps more than we cared to admit, and this uncertainty was what made our choices so important.

After feeding them dinner, I tucked them into bed. Then I paced. The loneliness and claustrophobia grew until I finally went outside to escape it. The night was creaking with crickets. The odor of fish was still lingering. It reminded me of a fish market I once visited in Senegal. The cul-de-sac was quiet and I sat on the porch feeling my stomach churn.

I thought about my old neighbor, Toke. She was a Navajo lawyer from Gallup. With her low ponytail and runner's physique, she was pretty and professional. We'd been instant friends, but after a few short months she and her husband began to complain about the uptight mood of West County people.

"Think about your job benefits! Treat it like an exotic experience!" I said, but my advice to live with a traveler's attitude didn't make sense.

"Missouri isn't exotic," she said, laughing.

When she and her husband moved back home, Simone reminded me that neither of them had ever traveled. They simply weren't adventurous. I nodded without admitting that I knew how Toke felt. Missouri was a foreign version of the same America. It was different but still connected in history, forgetful and overlooking in its gaze. It offered a viewfinder Toke and her husband didn't want because it made them feel invisible.

I went to the backyard and looked at our overgrown flower bed. I knelt down and started weeding by moonlight. Thinking of the turtles, I ripped and tore at the invasive plants. I always said the revolution was seeking to understand foreign people in foreign places. But the idea didn't feel smart or noble anymore. I was losing my faith.

It had been a rough month. Simone had turned down a job offer in Seattle where my younger sister lived. Two weeks before, I'd learned that I was pregnant. On the brink of stepping out of my role as a full-time mother, with my youngest son starting kindergarten in the fall, I had painted myself back into a domestic corner. It felt like an utter setback, yet who could I blame? Did I really want to resent my own child, a baby I was sure to love? Hearing Simone's truck in the driveway, I brushed my hands clean of soil and dirt and went to greet him.

The following week, geologists would come to study the sinkhole. They would attend a neighborhood association meeting and explain the faulting of the earth's crust beneath the lake bed. We would learn that our two adjacent neighborhoods, Lake Chesterfield and Port of Nantucket, had been built on a long narrow fissure. They would explain that the water's weight, over time, had shifted a large boulder and an entire shelf had crumbled into an underground cavern with the lake water behind it.

The geologists said they could dig and fill in the rift, plug it with concrete or rock, but there was no guarantee it would hold forever. The ensuing neighborhood association minutes were filled with arguments about God's plan. Some people said the area should be returned to grass and woods, perhaps with a park at the narrow end away from the sinkhole, but the people in favor of restoring the lake won the argument. Since the lake technically belonged to the Lake Chesterfield Association, and we lived in Port of Nantucket, I didn't get to be involved. I simply passed the area and dreamt of how to get out of the suburbs.

Sometimes, late at night, I walked over to the shore and sat, contemplating the exposed site until it was finally fixed.

Summer Night Rain— St. Louis

JOHN HICKS

Again tonight, early dark descends in smell of rain.
The street rises; traffic eases. Quick breeze

rattles attention from my blinds; their rigging clatters.
Big drops. Fatter. Faster. Then the downpour.

Waiting on his dog, a man stretches his shirt over his head,
peers through the collar. The dog watches back.

First floor spotlights lift the facade across the street
scaling masts white with rain. The wind changes.

I lower my windows against the spray. We turn into the wind.
Sails fill; the hull creaks. We're heading into autumn.

Consuming Fires

SAMUEL AUTMAN

I was fourteen years old the first time I spoke in tongues.

Rev. Dunlap, a light-skinned, curly-headed man and associate minister at San Francisco Temple Church of God in Christ had called audience members to come up and receive prayer near the end of a week-long revival meeting in the summer of 1982. Seated next to Randy and Paul, two friends from Boy Scout Troop 150 at Scullin Elementary School, I got up. I had grown tired of West Galilee Missionary Baptist's funereal services, where my mother forced me to attend. God had to be more exciting. Her sister, Aunt Freddie Mae, and her quiver of twelve kids demonstrated that although sanctified folks followed strict rules, they embodied a kindness I attributed to their religious upbringing. I wanted to be like them, so I was searching.

Before I realized it, I had walked up to the front of the sanctuary and stood with a handful of seekers at the altar. One of the ministers—I don't remember who—prayed fervently that God would touch me. With my eyes shut and head bowed, my soul broke open with anticipation. I waited for a few minutes to feel something. Nothing. Soon the minister walked away. I glanced at the empty church aisle on the right and began walking back to my seat. As I made my way down the aisle, a woman in a long Laura-Ingalls-Wilder-*Little-House-on-the-Prairie*-type dress, who appeared to be in her late twenties, met me halfway. At about five feet, seven inches, the dress was quite plain. Her hair was pulled up in a bun. She pressed her hand on my forehead and started speaking in tongues machine-gun style, a rapid Spanish or Portuguese-sounding language. I paused, closed my eyes as if to pray and fell over laughing. Syllables, a mixture of words and phrases I had heard other people saying, plus new ones, bubbled out of my mouth. I thought of a word in tongues and then it leapt off my lips. I wasn't forcing it. My tongue was caught somewhere between being the pen of a ready writer and a being bridled by a horse trainer. Both things were happening. I did the speaking and something enabled me. All the while, a warm, joyous presence poured over my body. Inside I wondered what Paul and Randy thought, yet it didn't matter as a joyous bubble rose from within and washed over me. In a few minutes, the sensation lifted. I went back to my seat. As those old saints used to say, I knew in my knower that the fire of God had touched my body and soul. I felt light-headed as I walked out of the church with my friends, confident that I had partaken of a heavenly secret they hadn't tasted—one powerful enough to snuff out the fire smoldering in my genitals.

When Paul wrote to the Ephesians not to be drunk with wine but filled with the spirit, he could have meant people in north St. Louis, where a liquor store stands across the street from every church. For a year we lived on the 4300 block of Shreve Avenue, directly across from the grand Saint Engelbert Catholic, right down the street from West Galilee Missionary Baptist Church, a storefront where my family attended. By 1982, San Fran became my drug of choice. San Francisco Temple Church of God in Christ on San Francisco Avenue was one of many COGIC congregations bearing the name "Temple," such as Bostick Temple, Shiloh Temple, Kennerly Temple, and Kossuth Temple. All these churches were on the north side.

COGIC (ko-jek) stands for the Church of God in Christ, a predominantly African American organization founded in 1897 that is one the nation's largest Christian denominations. They are Protestants who believe in sin, salvation through Jesus Christ, baptism, resurrection from the dead, eternal judgment, and the gifts and manifestations of the Holy Spirit, which they call the Holy Ghost. The speaking in tongues, healings, and all manner of miracles in their doctrine are in line with the New Testament book of Acts. They also adhered to the old-fashioned holiness codes. Women were forbidden from wearing pants or makeup, men weren't supposed to put on shorts. Drinking, cursing, and smoking were considered sinful, too. Sanctified means set apart, holy. But, too often the rules made them just cranktified.

A few days before I turned fifteen in August 1982, I put on a pressed shirt, slacks, and tie and walked to San Fran with the idea it would be my new church home. Sunday morning services functioned like theater. The preachers, choir members, mother's board, deacons, and ushers played their parts. The musicians, which included an organist, pianist, both bass and lead guitarists, and drummers functioned as interactive orchestra. When the energy hit a high note, any member of the audience could jump on stage.

On that first Sunday when the organ and tambourines crescendoed at the peak of testimony service, my body sprang to the floor. First I spun around, danced between two pews, and then near the wall as if stomping roaches. In my mind, I was only partially in charge of those spontaneous moves. God himself served as the puppet master and I, the sacred marionette, moved to the holy beat. For a few seconds I wondered how I looked to the other saints but I remembered, I was in a sanctified church, dancing before the most high God! Never had I enjoyed such freedom of movement as I twirled to the music. Jesus lived in my heart. The fire of the Holy Ghost consumed my body. The Son of God had set me free and I was free indeed. I was sanctified! Justified, chosen of God and nothing was going to stop me in life. The moment lifted. I sat back done. I was hooked. In moments such as those, the kindling of sexual desire felt defeated, squashed even. I concluded that the fires of the spirit had made me heterosexual. I had become a zealot with a secret struggle.

While the fires of the spirit were consuming my mind, my genitals were smoldering. As each day passed, it became clearer that I was gay. Males wrestling on TV in spandex made me sexually aroused. The bodies excited me more than the sport. Homosexuality was the biggest sin in the sanctified churches. A prostitute, drug addict, or alcoholic, which they called drunks, could get saved and become good Christians. Saints looked side-eyed and chuckled when Jerry, the notorious ex-homosexual, put his hands on his hips and said during the testimony service that he was, "now saved and sanctified and no longer a homosexual." It seemed like he was lying because he was so queenie. I never talked to him.

When many teenaged boys were driving cars, engrossed in sports and chasing girls, I chased God. I took notes during every sermon. If someone quoted a Bible verse or an idea like "Deliverance comes on the wings of praise," I scribbled that in my notebook. San Fran had so many different kinds of people, preachers, and activities, I lost myself buying tapes and books and lost myself in a sea of missionary's (women's) service, prayer meeting, Bible study, youth service, and junior and senior choir rehearsal. I thought to please God I had to do all of that, simultaneously keeping me out of the house where my sister's mental illness made life intolerable. With all of the church activities, my grades were suffering.

Not long after I turned sixteen, I sought the pastor's guidance on time management. In his "baby saints" class he told us his door was always open to help new Christians. I took him up one Sunday night after YPWW, which stood for Young People Willing Workers and functioned like evening Sunday school for high school and college-aged kids. We met in his study with the door closed. Elder Mac towered with his darker-skin, withered face, bulbous nose, and a shiny bald head. Patches of his hair that his wife, a beautician, had chemically treated, slapped from the side and to the back of his head when he stood behind the podium preaching. Droopy eyes revealed a man who had either spent his pre-sanctified years drinking or who had insomnia. Elder Mac pushed his glasses up on his nose and asked me to sit next to him.

"I'm worried about not having enough time to pray and read the Bible," I said.

"How often do you pray?" he asked as he leaned into an opened Bible.

This was my first time meeting in private with Elder Mac. I considered him a holy man. In person his voice was softer than I expected.

"I pray every day for a few minutes before I go to bed. I'd love to know how to pray and read the Bible. I just can't find the time."

He reached into his dark wooden desk and pulled out a small piece of paper and began to scribble.

"What time do you leave to go to school?"

"At about 6:30 in the morning. I'm back by 3:00 in the afternoon."

He wrote that down.

"What do you do after that?"

"I have a paper route. I deliver newspapers until about 5:00 or 5:30."

He scribbled again.

"And after that?"

"My mother makes dinner. We're usually done by 6:30."

I glanced at his hand. He wrote a grid of my daily schedule.

"From 7:00 until 10:00 p.m. I relax and watch TV. I finish my homework before going to bed."

He looked at me through his glasses. "That's your problem right there, young man. You're watching too much television when you could be praying and reading the Bible for at least two hours every night. You could get your homework done in an hour."

The schedule map looked clear. He was right. I felt embarrassed because I was watching a lot of television. But Elder Mac didn't factor in my other distractions: all of the church activities. Once a month I attended youth nights on Mondays. Tuesdays we had church-wide prayer meetings. Wednesdays the "missionaries" met (code speak for women who he didn't let speak behind the podium, so they met in the basement). Thursdays they had ministers' night. Friday night Elder Mac led Bible study. Saturday was youth choir rehearsal. My biggest conflicts were trying to decide if I should study, attend Bible study, or watch *Dallas*, on CBS. I almost always skipped Thursday night preaching so I could watch *Knots Landing*. The sex scenes between Gary Ewing and Abby were too steamy to miss. Gary was J. R.'s brother from *Dallas*.

"How well do you know Chris?" Elder Mac asked.

"I know him from school."

"Did you know that young man has been tarrying to receive the Holy Ghost?"

"I know he's been tarrying to get the Holy Ghost. We go to the same school."

"Do you and him hang out a lot?"

"Not really. Sometimes I see him on the bus."

"Well, you're the reason he can't get the Holy Ghost. I know what you and he are doing. That's not pleasing to the Lord! All fornication is sin before God. You can't play two ends against the middle, young man. You can't have two masters. You either serve God or you fall into pleasing your flesh."

"I'm not doing anything with Chris, Elder Mac."

He looked at me with such disgust. I had become the most abominable of the young people. The accusation was a double gut punch because it was false. I hadn't done anything sexual with Chris, or with anybody at that point. Elder Mac had accurately discerned my struggle with homosexuality. I felt so exposed.

The eighth chapter of Saint Luke tells the story of a woman who spent all her money trying to get healed by physicians from a continual bleed. By the time she came to see Jesus, she had been bleeding for twelve years. According to the Biblical account, she had been whispering to herself, "If I can touch the hem of his garment I will be made whole." The story says when she pushed through the crowd, she touched him with enough force that he said, "Who touched me?" Once he saw her he pronounced that her faith had made her whole.

No doubt Elder Mac saw me walk over to McDonald's with Chris to get a Big Mac. One time I stood at the altar and prayed with him as he waited to receive the Holy Ghost. That was it. Chris and I weren't close. This was the first time anyone had tried to shame me on something I wasn't doing, and I was disappointed. Indeed, homosexuality *had* taken root in my imagination. But Elder Mac's observation became its water and sunlight. Did occasional fantasies mean I was playing two ends against the middle? I was so conflicted and blindsided by his accusation.

God's house was no longer safe. The embrace of saints who seemed to love me vanished in that moment. That Elder Mac had somehow accessed my secret thoughts stymied and petrified me. Did I look like one of those church sissies I had seen at San Fran, closeted gay men who hid behind their wives? I had heard whispers about an associate minister who had been accused of touching a teenage boy. Years later I got the story from that boy, who had grown into a gay man. We sat in a bar in the Central West End and he told me all of the details. If Elder Mac, God's man who spoke in tongues from the pulpit, his body shaking with Jesus' resurrection power, couldn't see that I was innocent, then what was true in the sanctified church?

Deep in the inner recesses of my soul, I came to church in part to keep those feelings in check. Was it not working? Had God failed? Why had God revealed my innermost thoughts to my pastor? Wouldn't God let him know I was not acting on those feelings?

I left his office crushed. The holiest man I knew believed I was either a liar or a practicing homosexual or both. I didn't have any practice back then. Embarrassment became rage. All my life I had gone to black churches, sang in choirs, heard and adored black preachers. I was too young and unformed to know, but Elder Mac had singed me. A few months later, I stopped attending San Francisco Temple.

One of the sweet saints, Sister Dunlap, who had been our Sunday night youth Bible teacher, reached me by phone at home after I had several missed weeks of church. She said the Lord had healed her of breast cancer.

"I haven't seen you in church for a while Brother Sam. I just wanted to check and see if everything was all right."

"Oh, I'm fine. I'm just busy with schoolwork. I'll be back," I lied.

I didn't know it then, but Elder Mac was my last black pastor and San Francisco Temple my last black church. The false accusation bounced me out for good but I was far from off the spiritual pathway. Years later, as a man in my early thirties, when I worked as a reporter for the *St. Louis Post-Dispatch*, I got assigned to do a story on what had become the San Francisco Complex, now in the northern St. Louis suburbs. I was intrigued to see how the church had changed and if Elder Mac would remember me.

I got in the car with Elder Mac and he drove me around, showing off the new buildings he had acquired: a nursing home for the senior citizens, a school where young black children learned Greek and Latin. I wondered if he recognized the face of the boy he had crushed fifteen years prior. It was clear he didn't. Although I had pushed hard to do the story as a way to make peace with the memory, the editors didn't bite. By then it didn't matter.

My last interaction with Elder Mac had been peaceful.

By the time Elder Mac died in 2010, he had withdrawn from the COGIC organization and started his own private school, a nursing home, and a bookstore. While his church shed some of the old-fashioned ideas, that did not extend to gay people. Homosexuality was expected to be crucified with Christ. For years my sexuality and spirituality wrestled with one another as serious opponents until I relaxed into the idea that the Jesus of the Bible hung out with outcasts.

It took me years to realize that everybody sees God through a glass darkly. They're entitled to their beliefs. As for me, the Lord is my shepherd and he knows I'm gay. That's all that matters now.

The accident

jason vasser-elong

Tumbling down Pernod Avenue, a white car sped dangerously toward the hospital, a woman in labor about to bring a baby girl into a cold world on a hot day in August. Without room to maneuver, the car smashed into other cars, not just mine, on its descent down a mountainous city street in the wee hours of a Tuesday morning. Before the light of day, while those working at a neighborhood café tied their aprons around tired hips that had yet to feel the thrill of a day's work, their legs balanced on already tired feet.

He forgot to turn his headlights on, but managed to stop at the stop sign, his tires skidding; leaving black war wounds next to my driver's side mirror, broken into pieces of a dream that i wished it was, when i discovered the debris. No note, no apology, just the cry of a baby coming into a reckless world, almost sure of leaving her to question why.

The Jordanian Kids

LAYLA AZMI GOUSHEY

I don't remember when I first heard about the Jordanian kids. My husband, Naser, who managed a gas station in South City at South Jefferson and Utah Street, probably mentioned them as an afterthought. Many immigrants live in South City: Bosnians, Vietnamese, Somalis, Eritreans, Arabs, Latinos, Ghanaians, and others. I only visited the station a couple of times per month, and I often lost track of the regular customers. There was a stretch of time during that summer of 1998 when the neighborhood boys were involved in a ruckus, and one boy brought his bike into the store and stayed there for over an hour because he was afraid to ride home by himself. The station's part-timer, Mike, finally retrieved his own bike out of the storage room and rode home with the boy because he felt sorry for him. I don't think this was one of the Jordanian boys, but the neighborhood battle must have brought them into the orbit of the gas station, which was a sort of neutral territory where the kids could all stock up on sodas and candy bars.

I do remember the day I heard about the girls. Naser had seen them playing along the South City street for a few weeks but had not realized they were the boys' sisters. The girls were four and six years old. They played along the busy street all day long. When they finally made their way to the station, Naser told them they shouldn't be out by themselves. He asked them to bring their father so he could meet him. The girls were talkative. They said they'd lived in the United States for two months and had already forgotten how to speak Arabic. They were very serious about this fact, even though they held their entire conversation in Arabic.

When the father arrived later that week, Naser and his coworkers lectured him. They told the father his kids needed to be in school; the girls shouldn't walk that far from their apartment; that someone might kidnap them. They told him to hire a babysitter. The father was an openhearted but naïve man. He told them his life story in a matter of minutes. He was divorced; he lacked significant job skills; he spoke very little English, and he came to the United States from Jordan that year because he thought he could do something better with his life than he had done so far. He appeared to want some kind of guidance. In fact, I am sure he expected it.

We moved to St. Louis from Dallas because of the gas station. Naser's friend had purchased the run-down property, and he was looking for a manager to take over its day-to-day operation and to also guide its renewal. The owner's brother-in-law also worked there, as did the owner's distant cousin, along with a local man who worked part-time. It was a family-run operation. This meant working hours were flexible, but significantly longer than the average workweek. The men who worked full time worked six days a week, for ten hours a day, for a predetermined salary. The pay was decent, although the job was a lot of responsibility. We were not blood relatives with the station owner, but the owner and Naser considered each other to be like brothers, and the owner's family embraced us as kin as soon as we arrived in St. Louis.

Naser and the other full-time workers were devout Muslims who prayed regularly. At certain intervals during the day, the men took a few moments to go back into the storeroom of the gas station, wash their hands and face, place a clean rug or even clean cardboard on the floor, remove their shoes, and begin praying. The prayer requires believers to stand and read a relevant portion of the Koran aloud (their choice), then kneel and touch head to the floor, reciting a short statement affirming God's benevolence. Worshippers repeat this process twice or more depending on the prayer time. Islamic prayer benefits worshipers' health, because they wash their hands, face, and feet five times a day. They also benefit from the spiritual meditation and movement during a busy workday. In this way the stresses of life are regulated, and faith and action become one. This simple but powerful ritual institutes a soothing and reaffirming rhythm of life.

The father of the Jordanian kids expected advice, not charity, and advice is something Arabs freely give. Arab people benefit from the collectivist practice of a constant give and take of information and advice. The give and take conversation is a bonding and learning activity. For any problem, someone has a success story, a parable, or a cautionary tale to offer for guidance.

Equally, frequent exchanges of information happen based on what *should* be done or the *best way* to do something. When I was young, I used to take umbrage at some of these suggestions. Virtual strangers offered me advice such as what I should study in school so I could make the best income, where I should work to have the best benefits, who is the best man to marry, or who I should talk to for the best of this or that. I also encountered questions about why I couldn't speak Arabic like a native, why I waited until college to learn to read Arabic, why I didn't practice a religion, why I didn't go to the *belad*, the old country, more often, or the most infuriating: *why didn't your father teach you anything about being an Arab?* Sometimes I would think: who do they think they are? They have *some* nerve. I was building my life on my terms. I knew I wasn't as clueless or superficial as they assumed.

The men at the station, including Muslim cabdrivers who stopped by daily for gas, cigarettes, and conversation, took the single father under their wing. One of them asked around and found a better job for the man. His salary did not increase in actual dollars, but his hours were shorter, and he was closer to his apartment. Soon after he began his new job, he started looking for more part-time work. The situation with his children remained unaddressed. They still roamed the street at will. The men at the gas station could not convince the father that, although children were safe to roam the street in their Jordanian hometown, they were not safe in their new environment.

The father of the Jordanian kids was decidedly attached to his children, but he was enduring trying and chaotic times, and he was neglecting their welfare. He said he tried to get them to go to school, but they didn't like it. They didn't understand what the teachers were saying. Several people offered to go with him to discuss the situation with a school counselor. Finally, he met with the counselor, and the three older children began to attend classes. The father hired a neighbor, a stay-at-home mom, to babysit the younger girl. But once in a while, someone saw the older kids playing on the street when school was in session.

The girls needed clean clothes, shampoo, and new shoes. We made arrangements for the father to bring them to our house so I could teach them how to use shampoo and so we could get some new clothes for them. That weekend I cleaned the apartment from top to bottom, rented children's videos, bought extra groceries, new blankets, and no-more-tangles shampoo. Naser waited for the father at the station a bit past quitting time. The plan was for the father to follow him home, go with us to Kmart if he chose, and stay overnight if he chose. We were now committed, fully concerned. Naser waited for over an hour. Then the father called. They had decided not to come. Thanks anyway.

When I learned the Jordanian kids would not be visiting us for the weekend, I was disappointed, and I also suppressed an urge of irritation.

How could a father who was in such desperate need not want his kids to benefit from us? We wondered: was he reluctant to accept charity? Did he feel he was giving over his parental power to us? We did not consider what we were doing as an act of charity, although, admittedly in hindsight, I was hoping to have some power and influence on the girls' lives. However, our main purpose was to establish friendship, to be of help in a small way, although our resources were limited.

But trouble was closing in. Around this same time, a young Bosnian girl who lived in the same area was taken from her house in the middle of the night by a neighbor. Her body was found several days later. Police determined she had gone willingly with her assailant and that he may have represented himself as a government official in his effort to get her out of the house.

On Monday, we learned bad fortune also had come the Jordanian family's way over the weekend. The rooms where they had been staying had caught fire. One of the boys, the eight-year-old, had broken his leg when he fell through a hole in the floor caused by the fire. They were temporarily out on the street, but the father had found a new ramshackle rooming house and preparations were already underway to move the family there. I was angry they had not called us. We were willing to be of service. I imagined the kids were traumatized.

The final blow occurred later that week. The father came to the gas station with a letter from Child Protective Services. He couldn't read it and asked someone to translate it for him. It said based on an inquiry from a concerned citizen, they requested he meet with them to discuss issues related to his children's welfare. The father did not take this letter as seriously as we did. We feared if events continued in the same manner, the children would end up in the foster care system.

After the fire, the Jordanian kids became a topic of conversation between several grocery storeowners, clerks, and cab drivers in the area. They made it their business to tell the father he needed to make sure his kids stayed in school. And the kids, especially the little girls, everyone agreed, needed their mother.

American media often portray Arab women, especially Muslims, as backward or oppressed. Some portrayals I have seen border on caricature. Certainly, Arab culture possesses patriarchal attitudes, many of which I have encountered, but Arab women exhibit many strengths within the culture.

They lead individual lives as rich and varied as women anywhere in the world. Opportunities for Arab women increase with social class, wealth, and political stability. Over the past one hundred years, Western military action and homegrown political repression has stifled the advancement of Arab peoples. True, not all Arab women have educational or career opportunities due to war and displacement, but in most of those cases neither do the men.

Sympathies for the Jordanian family continued to deepen, and some suggested the father take his kids back to Jordan. Maybe they could live with their grandparents or their mother until the father got on his feet. Four kids were too much for him to handle all on his own. The father agreed. Cabbies and clerks around the area began raising money to send the kids back to Jordan. There was never a question whether or not the matter was of their concern. One man even wrote a speech about the children's plight that he later gave after Friday prayers at the mosque. The children had become known in the area, and another store had independently come to the same conclusion as our group. They also started a fund to send the children home to family members. When word got around that there was more than one group of fundraisers in the area, those in charge of each fund contacted the other and agreed to combine the monies raised. New friendships were born as a result of the community effort. Minor feuds were set aside as interest in the welfare of the children grew and the desire for news overrode the importance of petty resentments. And the men who stood and worried about the family's fate day after day were not all Arabs, although most, except one who was Rastafarian, were Muslim. Some were Pakistani, Somali, Eritrean, or from another Muslim-African country. There was the sense, even among the single men, that the children could be their children, that the father could be one of them.

Most of the women I knew did not involve themselves in the problem of the Jordanian kids. One woman sent some clothing to them, another elderly woman offered to watch them while the father worked. Mostly, the women who were aware of the problem were busy with their own children, and while they spoke of the Jordanian kids in sympathetic tones and offered suggestions, they did not directly involve themselves.

As for me, I had no children at that time. As I think about it now, I was motivated to help because I recognized myself in those kids, especially the girls. My own upbringing was fraught with cultural confusion and tension. My father was a Palestinian immigrant and my mother was Anglo and American-born. Their rivalries and arguments scared and troubled me in my youth, and I had to learn to navigate their competitive temperaments while experiencing my own adolescent muddles. I thought if the Jordanian kids could go back to Jordan, where they could find themselves within one culture, they would be whole and healthy and ready to experience American culture when they were older. I wanted them to feel loved. I specifically wanted them to benefit from the love and influence of strong Arab women such as I had with my own Palestinian grandmother. This would help them develop cultural confidence and avoid the cultural confusions of the diaspora.

However, I had another reason for helping the Jordanian kids: their immediate health and welfare. It had to do with a story one man told of the two girls. The man had gone to visit the father, and without their knowledge, the girls had gone into the kitchen and prepared Arabic coffee, the thick sweet demitasse variety, in a pot on the gas stove. The oldest one stood on a chair over the open flame to do it. They also cut an apple into jagged slices and arranged it in a swirl on a saucer. They poured juice into glasses. Then, they brought out the coffee, the juice, cookies, and the apple hors d'oeuvres. The coffee was uncooked and tasted bitter, the apple slices were brown and arranged haphazardly, but they had acted with true Arab hospitality. It was a cute story, but I was dismayed they had used the stove. I was also concerned they were taking on adult responsibilities and falling into traditional female roles while already in a situation of limited economic options. Still, their impulses were guided by something. They wanted to please their father. I guessed they had learned hospitality from their mother and other members of their family.

I started to feel sorry for that unseen mother. Yes, it would be tragic if the children became embroiled in the foster care system, but even if they weren't, if they stayed in the US, they would be influenced by Western mores. Whatever understanding they had with their mother would dim. Many people experience gaps in understanding between themselves and their parents, but a cultural gap is something more. It cuts a deeper swath between generations. I imagined the kids would someday adopt a negative view of Arab women and men through Western eyes.

I began calling agencies for information. I called the Jordanian Embassy and asked for information about helping Jordanian children who get caught up in the foster care system. Was there a way to notify the family back home? The embassy representative was kind but not very helpful. He asked for the name of the man and his hometown in Jordan. I was wary of giving out too much information so I dodged his question. I did not want to begin a snowball effect wherein some bureaucratic clause would revoke the man's right to emigrate because of his plight.

What I saw in the future of the Jordanian kids was a fate worse than a temporary stay in the foster care system. I saw the cultural confusions they would someday face without the involvement of two committed parents. I saw that someday the father would realize his kids did not understand their heritage, his past, or the struggles he went through that allowed them to flourish. I feared they might someday, like me, come to resent how Arab people advised them that they should have kept up with their language and religion, and that their father had failed them in this regard. They would sit in movie theaters with their friends and pretend killing the Arab bad guys on film was cool. Or worse, they would endure media-horrors like Gulf War I and II, where we witnessed a flourishing Arab country and its people be decimated to punish its leader, or more accurately, to control the flow of oil resources from the Arabian Gulf.

After the Bosnian girl's fate was known—she had been kidnapped and killed—the intent to help the Jordanian kids intensified. Airplane tickets were very expensive and while donations were coming in, they only averaged between twenty-five and fifty dollars, which was quite a sacrifice for some who donated. Most who donated worked for low wages and had to support their own wives and children. Finally, a few well-to-do shop owners went ahead and made up the difference.

The week the kids were supposed to leave was an eventful one. The father agreed they should be sent back, and he said his brother's family had agreed to take them. Their mother lived nearby. The catch was the brother needed a monthly stipend to help with their care, as he already had children of his own. Coming off of the heady feeling of success that the plan had worked, the brother's demand seemed dour and petty at first. Eventually, it was seen as a logical demand, for the brother and his wife would have to see to the children's food, clothing, and education, not to mention housing them when they already had children of their own. The father agreed to send a monthly stipend to his brother. Finally, after a few snags were cleared up, the children were sent back to Jordan.

A few months after the Jordanian kids went back to Jordan, the father remarried. The kids wanted to come back and live with him. Plans were in the works to bring them back. I was astonished. I felt this was exactly the wrong thing to do. Almost everyone else I talked to disagreed with me. They figured as long as the kids lived in a stable environment with a parent or family member, where they lived mattered very little.

The motivations of most of the individuals concerned about the children originated from the same reasons as mine. We wanted to help. We wanted to do good. We were all seeing a bit of ourselves in the plight of that family. The difference was that my aims were more specific than theirs. Everyone else was content with the way things had turned out, and I finally had to accept the outcome. I realized I was not trying to save them, but save myself. I was trying to resolve my own complex feelings about my cultural belonging by steering their lives in a direction I wished for myself. To closet the kids in one culture, even if it was easier on them, would mean going against their wishes to be with their father. I was trying to alter a fragmented future that had already arrived.

As new events crowded into our lives, I all but forgot about the Jordanian kids. When I think of them now, I feel contrite. For some reason, I had assumed I knew best, my experiences would always match theirs, I could plan their lives, and my efforts could remove one portion of the hurts they must already be carrying in their hearts. I had demonstrated the same advice-giving, communal impulses I had once resented.

The Jordanian kids blew across the earth like seeds in the wind. Who was I to determine where they would take root? I hope they someday know their presence settled feuds, renewed forgotten acquaintances, and created new friendships.

Now, as their experiences join with others in this effort to untie the multicultural Gordian knot, I am chastened. I wonder how I could have assumed I should determine their fate? Who did I think I was? I really have *some* nerve.

Thought Two

MAJA SADIKOVIC

I opened the weather
app and typed Berlin
my favorite aunt
lives there, moved
back because she was a
lesbian, I wanted to compare
here and there, I typed Prijedor just
to find it auto
correct to some city in
Croatia, is my city not
worthy of a spot on a weather
app, is my sadness
irrelevant
but there was a genocide there
an afterthought came

Refugee Money

UMAR LEE

"The Serbs, they took the imam, they told him put up three fingers for the Trinity! The Bosnian imam refused and held up one finger and shouted *la ilaha illalah*! The Serb Crusaders slaughtered him."

The fiery Syrian imam was now crying in front of the crowd at the Islamic Center in Midtown. The mosque erupted into shouts of "*Allahu Akbar.*" Tears were flowing in the room. A middle-aged woman of Pakistani heritage, who I knew to be a doctor, stood up and promised to donate $10,000 to help Bosnians. Other women got up and started taking off jewelry to donate to the cause.

It was 1994. The Bosnian War was in full force. I was broke. Barely had the bus money to take the damn near two-hour journey from North St. Louis County that would take twenty minutes in a car. There was really nothing I could do for Bosnia at this point other than pray. Some local Muslims were going to attend a national rally supporting Bosnian Muslims in Washington, D.C. Famous Muslims, like Imam Siraj Wahhaj from Brooklyn and Imam Jamil al-Amin (formerly known as H. Rap Brown) from Atlanta would be speaking.

I had already missed the boat. My friend Ismail, another white American convert like me, had already gone to Bosnia and joined the foreign *mujahudeen* fighting to aid Muslims.

When I was on my *deen*, I would be in the classes with the Sheikh in the Walnut Park "Murderville" neighborhood of North St. Louis. The Sheikh and his students had rehabbed a vacant storefront building with three apartments in it. His students moved in from Oklahoma, Kansas, and Arkansas.

A native of Brooklyn, the Sheikh taught strict Islamic orthodoxy mixed in with things relevant to the lives of black people living in repressive conditions. His texts included books explaining the Quran, sayings of Prophet Muhammad, Islamic law, and prayer from scholars such as al-Albaani and Bilal Philips along with *The Wretched of The Earth*, *The Miseducation of the Negro*, and *The Autobiography of Malcolm X*.

The Sheikh would mix stories from the life of the Prophet with tales of growing up in Brooklyn or encounters with the police. He'd direct students to invite non-Muslim neighbors for dinner and tutoring sessions, and he'd send us out with nines and AK's to warn the gang-bangers to stay off our corner.

When I was with the Sheikh, his energy kept me on the straight and narrow. He specialized in reaching troubled young men and would say, "I come to the Bush for the Bushman." His right-hand man was a smooth-talking, gun-toting ex-pimp from St. Louis who'd fought with the *mujahudeen* in Afghanistan after converting to Islam. Both were skilled at talking to young men about their problems and getting them interested in seeing Islam as a solution to both their problems and those of society as a whole.

I would study the books and attend the classes and learn Arabic with the Sheikh, but that wasn't paying the bills. From time to time I'd dip away. Mostly working for temp services. You'd go downtown and sit in a crowded room at five or six in the morning to get called to go work in some factory. Normally I'd be the only non African-American in the room. Sometimes there'd be a couple of dingy looking white dudes.

When payday would come, temptation would arise. Not to buy drugs, because I didn't get high. The temptation would come to try and flip my money on the streets.

Big Hamp, an elder and mentor of mine, saw this. About my father's age, he knew more about the streets than I would ever know, and probably more than anyone of my generation would ever know. Big Hamp was born and raised in Kinloch. He had been shot on several occasions, stabbed, been in car wrecks, seen combat in Vietnam, been run over by a train, ripping a leg off, blown through a million dollars, been to prison for murder, and had both broken in and out of prison. On top of all that he was married to the sister of the former Pruitt-Igoe boss and gangster Fat Woods, and had been a friend of the legendary Grand Sheikh, Jerry Lewis-Bey.

"Save your money when you get paid. Don't try and flip it," Big Hamp told me one day as if he could read my mind.

I decided not to flip it, but I was still in need of more money. I had been making money with a baby formula hustle with Brother Mukhtar, a tall, light-skinned African American brother, and a group of Malaysian college students. The only problem was that I had dozed off one night in a crack house near the Kinloch-Ferguson border and gotten pistol-whipped and robbed. I needed money. I was trying to get the fuck out of lame-ass St. Louis and to a more vibrant Muslim community, like Brooklyn or northern Virginia.

It was during a trip to Kansas City that I'd been inspired by young brothers telling me about Brooklyn, Philly, and LA, where Muslim brothers had been robbing dope dealers. Their justification was that the companions of Prophet Muhammad had robbed the caravans of the *kufar* (disbelievers in Islam). Dope dealers were not only *kufar*, they were also doing damage to the community. Robbing them wasn't even stealing, it was just taken their ill-begotten money and doing something good with it.

So I hit a couple of licks in Kinloch. By the mid nineties the once thriving black community that had been a product of segregation and was surrounded by the formerly white communities of Ferguson and Berkeley had become lawless. The airport was buying up property and tearing down houses. Former residents who'd been there for generations were moving to previously white parts of North County. Entire blocks had become vacant or torn down. What was left was a lot of poverty, a thriving drug trade, a corrupt police department that was on the take and constantly making the news for scandals, violence, hustling of all manner, and a lot of churches in the mix.

My daughter's mother lived in the Boaz Apartments at "The Bottom" of Kinloch, as it was called. I'd see all kinds of white people driving into Kinloch to buy drugs. In the surrounding areas like Ferguson, they'd often get harassed by police, so many would buy their crack and then just get high in the car. Kinloch police busting them was never a concern. Occasionally St. Louis County police would come in for raids and major busts; but other than that, Kinloch was basically a Hamsterdam long before *The Wire*. My licks were robbing a few of the white people coming into buy crack. White people tended to scare easy anyway once they saw a gun. Robbing dope dealers, you may actually have to kill them to get their money, and even if you didn't, you still had to worry about retaliation. I chose the path of least resistance.

With a few dollars in my pocket I was ready to do some good with my money. A friend of mine named Brother Naji was working with a Muslim charity that had been set-up to help the new refugees coming to St. Louis. Naji represented a Malcolmesque tale of Islam totally transforming someone's life. In the 1960s and 1970s, he'd run the streets hard in East St. Louis and had been a member of the notorious "Metros" gang. His mother had actually been in the Nation of Islam when he was a child and attended the old Muhammad Mosque #28 on Grand and Cass. She died when he was young and he ended up running the streets and eventually serving fourteen years in prison for attempted murder and armed robbery. While in prison, Naji converted to Sunni Orthodox Islam under the leadership of Imam W. D. Mohammed (the son of the Honorable Elijah Muhammad).

From behind bars Naji got a college degree, became an imam, learned to read the Quran in Arabic, and read hundreds of books. Upon release from prison he began working for a dental company run by a white convert to Islam, and also worked helping Muslim refugees.

I told Naji to pick me up at Tomboy. In reality, the Tomboy store in Kinloch hasn't been called Tomboy in years. It was called King's Market and, like many North St. Louis City and County hood businesses, it was owned and run by Palestinian immigrants. These stores were controversial in the Muslim community. Many African American Muslims in particular were angry that Arab Muslims were in the black community selling things prohibited in Islam such as pork, alcohol, and lottery tickets. This particular store was in a building with a few other businesses, including a black-owned soul food restaurant and a place known as the "craphouse," where men gathered in a smoke-filled room to shoot dice on pool tables.

Naji didn't like Kinloch, but he picked me up anyway.

"Why don't you like picking me up in Kinloch?" I asked Naji from the passenger seat of his car.

"When I got out of prison I knew I could never carry a gun again. So before going anywhere I ask myself if I need a gun. If the answer is yes, then I don't go. Kinloch is a place where you need a gun," Naji said.

"So, do you like living out in North County?" I asked, knowing he'd just moved to the Lucas and Hunt Village apartments right off Highway 70.

"Yeah, you know, other than being in the joint, I've been in East St. Louis my whole life. When I got out of prison and saw State Street, I wanted to cry. Everything boarded up and abandoned. Looks just like a big Kinloch. Back in the day though? East Side was the place to be. Now it's just sad. So I'm diggin' the suburban thing for now."

"We going to see the Bosnians tonight?" I asked.

"Naw, you know they wanna give all of their attention to the Bosnians. Don't get me wrong, I'm cool with helping them, and we're all Muslims, but we can't forget about helping the Ethiopian and Somali refugees. They need help, too, and don't get the same attention," Naji said, jumping on I-70 headed to the city as we passed block after block of a formerly black neighborhood in Berkeley that had been torn to the ground by the airport.

"You know why," I said.

"You damn right I know, akh," Naji replied.

We drove about fifteen minutes through north St. Louis and then through downtown, getting on Highway 44 before getting off on Jefferson. Bosnians were mostly being settled in the previously white "south side hoosier" neighborhoods of Bevo and Dutchtown, but these areas were also seeing increasing numbers of black residents. Ethiopian and Somali refugees were being placed just south of downtown in higher-crime areas near public housing. An apartment complex near Jefferson and Chouteau had become their hub, with activity centering around Hickory Street.

Naji had grown fond of an Ethiopian Muslim family with four young daughters. He would go over to their house and the mother would cook traditional foods for him, and the kids would practice their English. I decided that I'd give the money I'd recently gotten from robbing white dopefiends in Kinloch to this family. At least a big chunk of it. Seemed like a great way to clean the money.

We pulled up on Hickory in front of their place. Naji had even brought a bean pie as a gift. No sooner than we tried to get out, we were surrounded by police. All of them white. Ordered to get out and put our hands on the car. We complied.

"Down here buying some dope tonight?" asked the cop who was doing all the talking.

"No," Naji answered. "We're Muslims. We aren't involved with all that. We are down here visiting refugees."

"If you're Muslim, what's the white boy doing with you?" the cop asked.

"He Muslim too," Naji said. The white cops started laughing. The cop then went through my pockets and found my money.

"Here to visit some imported niggers, huh? Well, what do you need this cash for? I think you're headed to see the dopeman. I tell you what, I'll leave you my card. If you can bring me a paycheck, I'll give the cash back. If not, I got my mind on a new fishing pole." The cops all laughed as they got back in their cars and drove off.

Seconds later we were inside the house of the Ethiopians.

"What happened?" we were asked in a thick east African accent.

"St. Louis happened," we both said. I added in, "Welcome to St. Louis."

An ode to Imo's

jason vasser-elong

i close my eyes &
it's a thin pillow
on the tips of my fingers /oregano
wafting   carried by the steam,
bending nearing my mouth—its square
snug between my lips—
teeth/then there it was
balancing on my tongue,

a gondola floating one shallow pond
or a thick blanket of spice coating my whole orifice

sending accordions through my entire body—
sending my lips and cheeks to the dance
painted in sauce, slathered in the Italy of a friend's dreams.

The Last Cricket of the Season

EAMONN WALL

When I catch a cricket's high
autumnal pitch sprung from
among a row of ragged junipers,
my heart seeks out the levelest
and most insistent, homeward
foot and yard to my front door.
On Missouri's warmest days,
these many free and careless
years, I have often paused for
shade under a great oak tree
to observe pairs of doves that
quietly group under this same
line of evergreens. My children
have grown and spread, my
sweetheart is at home stirring
alone a late martini, and cars
roar to the westward freeway
bound for glory and California:
I grow invisible or gray which
is just the same difference as
they say. But this cricket's call
rocks my world—Jimi Hendrix,
Rolling Stones. Though cold
and colder this evening's air, I
can still pitch high, and I can
swing homeward, as if immortal.

The Tour

LYNDSEY ELLIS

At twenty past 2:00 on Friday afternoon, my friend arrives at the woodsy ranch I've been temporarily staying at in St. Louis County.

"Excuse me, is this the right house? I'm looking for this girl . . ."

I throw my arms around him. He laughs, a chuckle that makes me ache with remembrance, as he breathes into my neck.

Still beaming, we unlock and assess each other. Even on an overcast day with clouds blotching the sky, and the air choked with an unexpected, but necessary, foreshadowing of rain, our burnt sugar brown complexions still match. So does the visual rhythm of our kinky hair—his, a beady box cut, mine, long and dreadlocked.

He's rounder, I notice, with the ease and straightforwardness that separates boys from men. Three electric gray strands stick out of his thick beard. I playfully pick at them, watching him realize that I'm rounder, too, mostly around the waistline.

We lollygag around the house for a while. He thinks I've done all right for myself, considering the transition back to my hometown. After thirteen years of living in the Bay Area, I returned to St. Louis in early spring, and despite being awarded a two-month writing residency to complete my first book, I'm still in between full-time jobs. I just purchased the first car I've had in four years. I'm single with no children.

A lot of people would say I'm failing. And although my life as an emerging writer has presented several rewarding and insightful experiences, it remains a challenge not to sometimes internalize this view, especially in between the highs. If anyone gets this, it's my friend—the poet who I've known and loved for over ten years, from West Coast to Midwest, virtually and in-person, once as a lover and now as one of my best friends.

We embark on a crash course tour of the city. Florissant. Ferguson. Normandy. Delmar Loop. Forest Park. Central West End. Midtown. St. Louis Place. Downtown. Tower Grove.

It dawns on me that I "get" my friend just as much as he "gets" St. Louis. Or, at least as much as he once thought he got it. Seething, I fly down I-70 west as he flits through his YouTube playlist of big booty girl freestyles and makes comparisons of St. Louis to other cities in between songs.

There are worse drivers here than in San Francisco and Michigan combined.

The White Castles remind him of that one time in Chicago.

Some apartment buildings resemble the housing projects in Memphis.

Those houses near Hyde Park—boarded up and held by crumbling brick—could be in Detroit.

All that foliage in Old Jamestown makes the place look like Cleveland.

The Underground Railroad on the Riverfront Trail comes close to the one in Atlanta.

Is the seafood or the jazz scene here as good as it is in New Orleans?

Do folks park their cars on the lawn here like they do in Mississippi?

By the time we meet my dad for lunch the next day at a Brazilian restaurant in St. Charles, I'm nearly numb with frustration and craving the solitude of my cubby-like studio back at the residency. My friend seems unfazed as he gets the lowdown on my most embarrassing childhood memories from the man who helped raise me.

The conversation veers to racism, or the youthful naiveté associated with the lack of it, when my dad recalls my first boyfriend: a four-year-old stubby white boy with a short temper named Ned who I kissed on the tire swing in day care. Later, in our pre-teens, we'd learn how uncool and potentially dangerous it was to speak to each other, let alone remain friends, in the hallways of Kirby Junior High (now Hazelwood East Junior High), a mildly segregated junior high school in so-called inclusive North County. I'd regret distancing myself after hearing of the motorist who fatally struck Ned on his bicycle near the corner of West Florissant and Old Halls Ferry Road, just blocks from our old day care center.

"Shame what happened to little Ned," my dad says, re-adjusting his cap. "Quite the character, if I ever saw one."

And then, just like that, he and my friend are accepting slices of the next meat display at our table—a Brazilian tradition—before exchanging horror stories of being a black man in the workforce, the problem with interracial dating, growing obesity in the Midwest, Farrakhan's teachings.

On our way back to Florissant to prepare for my aunt's wedding, I notice the change in my friend's attitude. He's more relaxed after the talk with my dad; a man, he says, who is his own man, living on his own terms. I'm floored by my friend's admiration of my father and the way it tempers his perception of St. Louis.

Finally, he lets the city breathe and be its own person. He listens deeply when I explain the reversed white flight back into the inner city as if gentrification is a new term he's not familiar with. He says the unpredictability of the weather here, oppressive humidity with sheets of hard rain and all, is a devastatingly pleasant experience. He sees the children with ringwormed scalps on their backyard trampolines and in their family's outdated above-ground swimming pools, their tongues stained from the dye of Jolly Ranchers, as springtime gems set in their messy, awkward ways.

He hears the big love and hard living in the throats of women who dot the pimples on their face with eyeliner to make them appear as beauty marks. The homegrown majesty of storefront churches, Chop Suey shops, and liquor marts with drive-thrus. Through my friend's eyes, I realize there are things I missed without realizing I missed them. Mostly, I missed the two-tonedness of St. Louis. The almost indescribable way things here never matched or could be boxed in.

"The land is citified," my mother explains to my friend after the wedding, "it's the people who are country."

At night, my friend and I sleep side by side with my laptop separating our bodies, the murmur of a Netflix film underneath our playful conversation. We're comfortable but careful. I ignore the tingle I still get when lying so close to him and remind myself of our failed romance: a blur of financial setbacks, petty fights, subliminal Facebook posts, drunk text messages, birthday cards to soften blows, confused and resentful silent spells, random longwinded phone calls—all the things that define two people once constantly on the cusp of lovers and pals.

With love, timing and circumstance has never been on our side. Instead of the marriage I'd hoped for, we got Harry-and-Sallied. It is what it is.

Under the ceiling fan's steady whir, I think of my hometown and how it's friend-zoned regularly—consistently allied but rarely taken seriously as a relocation choice or a tourist destination. How convenient it is for people to base their assumptions of St. Louis on their own lens of experience, and the media's wrongful flyover narrative of the Midwest.

I think about dead Ned, wondering if kids will ever have the willpower to stay colorblind, and lapse into a self-pity that questions God's sense of humor at killing the person who may have been my husband—my soul mate.

On Sunday, my friend drags out conversations over breakfast, mostly on his worries about juggling dead-end jobs with his art, to make up for how we might not see each other for another five years. It's my turn to listen deeply, so I do. Before he leaves, I hug him tightly and pretend I don't hear him say how glad he is to put St. Louis down as another place he's visited.

Breaking the Wheel

LISA AMPLEMAN

As a child, I lived
on St. Catherine Street,
patron saint of unmarried girls

and knife sharpeners,
spinsters, and spinners.
Strapped to a spiked wheel for torture

when she wouldn't
consort with the emperor,
she shattered it with her touch.

Impatient, the executioner
took her head instead.
At one end, St. Catherine Street

becomes Greengrass. In the middle,
we sledded down the front-yard hill,
whooping with joy or terror.

The street dead-ends
near Coldwater Creek
with its concrete banks and nuclear secrets:

runoff from radioactive waste
leeched into its water
decades ago. The kids who played

on its banks (my mother
never let me) have
salivary gland growths, thyroid tumors.

In one treatment, neutron therapy,
the radiation takes away
 from what it gave.

In the room, a "vault,"
photons bounce off a bit
of beryllium, and the tumor's DNA

dances in the ray,
cannot cope. The cell
breaks, defeated wheel.

For years, the official word
was: no link between
their illness and the creek.

Now the state sifts the soil.
Thorium lurks a few feet down.
Don't breathe it in,

the researchers warn;
no landscaping or tilling here.
Use caution. We can clean this up.

Caravaggio's Catherine holds a sword,
her dress sleeves white
against the dark shadows of her skirts.

The wheel is broken behind her,
two spokes with empty couplings.
An unbroken halo curves

around her head, barely there,
gold that might
float away on the lightest exhalation.

"Breaking the Wheel" was first published in Miracle Monocle *in 2018.*

City

jason vasser-elong

Under a canopy
maple leaves drape,

their branches bend brown
spines at the end of the song
of summer, and i am
surrounded,

embraced by the city
moving around me.

City traffic,
laughter of friends
in passing, the trickling
fountain nearby—

a welcome constant
in my life;

there are already leaves
on the ground

& right now
i am anticipating a hillside
or a lake that I have never seen,

and other unfamiliar scenic
treasures all of the pleasures
while vacationing
with my lover
who will eventually become my wife,

but for now, it's the light
touching the bricks
on the side of the building,

the symphony of sirens
that have lost their urgency
on a street i've come to know
by touch—

knowing the vagabond
by name; & i trust
that the sun
without fail, will lick
the whole west side of my
courageous city, fighting
within itself
it too finding the beauty within.

A Kinloch Perspective

STEVEN PEEBLES

The celebration of an ending can be a new beginning.

Cars lined the street as far as the eye could see. Music was drifting out of the church and into the street. This was reminiscent of days of old—people seeing faces that they had not seen in years. There were hugs and tears. No one quite knew what to expect. Nostalgia had taken over.

Even as the community around it changed over the years, the one thing that was a constant was the love that existed for Devotional Baptist Church, and for Kinloch itself. But despite that love, and despite the bittersweet nostalgia filling the pews, Devotional's structure at 5477 Rev. Earbie Bledsoe Sr. Street was about to share in the same demise as other parts of Kinloch.

I served as the emcee of this program, Devotional's final service in April 2015, which was a deep honor for me. The choir gave its rendition of "Jesus Will Take Care of Me," which was a silent theme that we embraced as our new beginning was upon us. Being the emcee gave me a chance to speak on a few key moments of our church's history. I told the story of when Pastor Bledsoe announced that we were going to enlarge the sanctuary because we had standing room only attendance on most Sundays back in the late 1970s and early 1980s. Those who recalled those times applauded. I also spoke about how the church was struck by a Molotov cocktail in 1985 after the first attempt to set the building afire failed. This was during the construction process. It was a trying time for the entire congregation, as the persons responsible are still unknown. But the resolve of the congregation could not shaken or broken.

We sang an all-time favorite song, "Old Landmark," led by Pastor Lance Peebles, my cousin and Devotional's long-time minister of music. The crowd stood and sang along with the choir. The Rev. Eugene Peebles was on hand, too, and he blessed us with the award-winning sounds of his saxophone.

Devotional Baptist Church was founded by the late Rev. Nathaniel Dunn in 1965. Pastor Dunn was succeeded by the Rev. Earbie Bledsoe Sr. Devotional thrived under the leadership of both pastors, with Pastor Bledsoe being partly responsible for the building of three sanctuaries with his own hands. I can recall our choir at one point in time being over one hundred members strong. The choir had recorded an album and was well-known throughout the Midwest. Devotional also was a favorite spot for evangelists to visit and preach the gospel. Rev. Dr. J. E. Turner and Rev. Cleophus Robinson Sr. are two that immediately come to mind. Devotional also had a long-standing radio broadcast on AM 920 WGNU, where the choir and preaching was featured.

Pastor Bledsoe, who grew up as a sharecropper in Tutwiler, Mississippi, took great pride in what was about to happen on that day in 2015. Still, he often speaks of those years on the cotton fields. Bledsoe, who is the seventh of thirteen children of Willie and Mozella Bledsoe, fondly reflects on the journey from those cotton fields to working in construction, to ultimately becoming a pastor. He stands about six feet, two inches, and is of slender build. It is difficult to image him swinging a large sledgehammer or packing large stacks of lumber. However, those moments lent themselves to the construction of Devotional's sanctuaries over the years.

Never one at a loss of words, Bledsoe chided those in attendance about a sharecropper having such a bountiful blessing placed upon him with the new construction about to happen. It is not uncommon for him to strike out in humor to prove a point. He is also well-known for his use of parables. His parables and anecdotes are legendary.

Bledsoe has always been a humble man and full of philanthropy. He has a community garden of fresh vegetables that he shares with his church members and folks of Kinloch and adjacent communities. Former Missouri Lieutenant Governor Peter Kinder acknowledged Bledsoe's philanthropy in April 2014, awarding him the Senior Service Award. This award speaks to the kind of person Bledsoe is. I am proud to be his nephew, and am appreciative of the example that he's set. Another such recognition of his presence and service in Kinloch was changing the name of the street where the church sat. In the summer of 2012, 5744 Monroe was renamed 5744 Rev. Earbie Bledose Sr. St.

I grew up in Kinloch, at a time when the stores and businesses seemed like they would be there forever. Uncle Dick's store on Scudder was one of them. That store was much like any other storefront, unassuming with the second floor serving as the owners' residence. Uncle Dick and Aunt Rose—Marion and Rose Smith, officially—treated their customers like family. Uncle Dick would always have a smile on his face and wore overalls. He would peer over the top of his glasses while sitting behind the counter and ask you for your order. Aunt Rose would be present and made sure that we kept in line and minded our manners. If you could commit a Bible scripture to memory, Uncle Dick would give you a piece of candy. Many would frequent this establishment for a made-to-order hamburger and to listen to the jukebox. Uncle Dick and Aunt Rose seemed like an extension of grandparents. Not only would they feed kids whether they had money or not, but they would also dispense wisdom, giving us words to live by: mind your parents, and go to church as often as possible. They would also impart on us the value of education.

Nelson Norris owned another store like this. Like Bledsoe, Uncle Dick, and Aunt Rose—and many in Kinloch—Mr. Norris believed in philanthropy. He, too, would issue credit to his customers without collateral. Freeze pops, potato chips, soda, gingerbread men with the red icing—these were among my favorite items to purchase. During the winter months or rainy days, Mr. Norris would open his doors for us while we waited on the school bus. Philanthropy, brotherly love, and family helped to keep the community stable in those times.

I remember Kinloch's fruit trees, too. Those trees meant that we could have a snack on the way from one place to another: apple, pear, peach, plum, along with muscadine grapes. We would fill coffee cans with mulberries and enjoy them, much like children of today enjoy gummy bears. We feasted on nature's candy.

The community was more like one big family, as everyone knew one another. People waved from their porches or would say to tell my parents hello. This refrain was repeated everywhere I would go. It was not an unusual occurrence to either knock on a door to ask for a cold glass of water or to simply turn on the hose for a quick drink. This sense of community is what Kinloch was all about, and always had been.

Kinloch's significance to the African American community derives from its historical roots. Many rumored that Kinloch was the oldest all-black established city in the history of the United States, which, while it has not been substantiated, strikes a chord with residents. Many of Kinloch's families originate from down South and came to Kinloch looking for a new life. Entrepreneurship became a way of life. Schools and churches sprung up left and right. New homes were built and roads were paved. The pride of ownership was reflected throughout the city, as well as in the core values of most families there.

Those streets, homes, and businesses are gone now, and so are most of the churches. Kinloch has changed from what was once a thriving residential area of roughly 14,000 residents to a mostly-vacant area of fewer than 200 residents. In the 1980s, Lambert International Airport was looking to expand, and Kinloch was part of those expansion plans. The buyout slowly eroded the tax base and the population began to drop. Some saw the buyout as a chance to start anew while others saw it as yet another infringement upon African American prosperity. Many residents had good paying jobs, working for places like McDonnell Douglas, Ford, Chrysler, General Motors, and Anheuser-Busch.

The people of Kinloch moved away, and most of the homes, stores, and churches were torn down for an airport expansion never actually happened. Deer graze where people once lived. The vacant lots left behind attracted drugs, crime, and poverty, giving Kinloch the reputation it has today—a reputation those of us who lived there hardly recognize.

In 2015, Devotional's leadership was contacted by developers who wanted to build on Kinloch's mostly-vacant land. They had agreed to build Devotional a new building in return for being able to demolish the current one to make way for a new one-million-square-foot warehouse, part of an ongoing plan to develop North County. We agreed.

As Devotional's new building was in its planning stages, there was one thought that permeated my mind: that our new edifice was going to be a monument to Kinloch, like an oasis in the desert. It would be a monument not just to the town itself, but to Uncle Dick, Aunt Rose, Mr. Norris, the fruit trees, the music, the churches, and everything else that made Kinloch what it was.

Those who came to be a part of this final celebration in April 2015 witnessed an awesome event. Not only was this building going to be raised, but our hopes and expectations for Kinloch's were to be raised as well. Funny how one word can represent two different things.

Every hymn sung by the church mothers, every prayer said by deacons on bended knees, helped to get us to this point. With the impeding demolition of Devotional, it was imperative to Pastor Bledsoe and our congregation to remain connected to the city we served faithfully. As the service went on, I recalled how the streets used to be full of people, heading to their respective places of worship.

Devotional may not look the same or even be in the same location—the new building was built in Kinloch on North Hanley Road. One thing that holds true about the new Devotional is that it is still full of the same type of love, joy, and community that made Kinloch special, even though Kinloch was razed, too. The new warehouse sits atop the Kinloch horizon, just below it sits Devotional Baptist Church. Each one is a new facility. Each one represents a new hope.

As the program was winding down, there were moments of smiles and tears. So many had hoped that this day would never come and others yearned for it. Pastor Bledsoe and I reflected upon the attendance of the program and the joy that was present. As one who had conflicted thoughts, I could not help but be thankful that Pastor Bledsoe would see yet another sanctuary be built, but this time never have to pick up a hammer. God is good!

In the Event of a Zombie Apocalypse

KELLY KIEHL DAVIS

for Mom, Dad, Andy, Sarah, Molly, and Erika

In the event of a zombie apocalypse, I would return to you, St. Louis. Do not worry. Although I have gone outside the 270 loop, that highway which constitutes the *real* St. Louis Arch, scooping the city between it and the Mississippi River like the curve of Yadier Molina's glove, it is really only you that I love. I have lived in cities with Riverfronts cleaner than our budget can afford; I have lived on the shores of the Great Lakes, in a state that names its school for buckeyes that grow in golden husks in the fields. Dear St. Louis, I am a planet of a beating heart that cannot escape the orbit of your love. I have lived nestled in the Blue Ridge Mountains and sat by camp fires in their forests, stringing daisy chains of mountain laurel, and I have lived minutes from the Mexican border, where I have gotten drunk on Cucumber Margaritas on the Fourth of July and worn paper flower crowns in my hair. St. Louis, I have lived by the Wisconsin prairie my Nordic ancestors first settled, where there are Willow Trees old as my great great grandma's gravestone and winters so cold you drink whiskey just to feel your fingers. Oh, St. Louis, I have lived all these places, but in the event of a zombie apocalypse, I would fight my way back to you. I would follow the esophagus of I-70 right into your rotting belly, because you, St. Louis, hold the jewels of the world, those few people with whom I would be honored to begin a post-apocalyptic commune among, in the humid, sticky basin of your love.

"In the Event of a Zombie Apocalypse" was first published in Contrary Magazine *in 2018.*

REALITIES

What We Live With, What We Live For

The Black Iron Fences of St. Louis

ASHER KOHN

The young man in jeans shifted his weight backwards, hands in the air and dreads down over his shoulders. It is August 2014, and he is trapped. Three police-soldiers in desert boots and gas masks are bearing down on him with weapons raised, looking like they just stepped out of one of the US's wars abroad. The man is pressed between them, the lens of photojournalist Whitney Curtis's camera, and a seven-foot high black metal fence in the background.

This particular fence is on the corner of Canfield and Florissant, but they are omnipresent in St. Louis, both the city and the county. There are the banks, grocery stores, and public parks that have their parking lots barricaded with these insurmountable (if rather stately) fences. But they mark more than just the places that demand protection. The fences also cut across streets and into livelihoods, trapping folks into situations from which there is no escaping a policeman's crosshairs or shorter life expectancies writ large.

St. Louis is built in brick, decorated in stone, and divided by seven-foot iron fences. These fences should be put in the outfield of Busch, sold in miniature at the Arch, and have children play on them at the City Museum. Their purpose is not to demarcate, but to remind passersby that they are not wholly welcome in the city their taxes pay for.

In 2011, I was first introduced to the fence on the corner of Skinker and Delmar, where it squared off a university-owned plot from people taking an eighty-foot shortcut through the grass. A few weeks after its installation, the police's nuisance abatement vehicle set up nightly watch at the gas station across the street—the snub-nosed mystery machine looking like a spring-loaded hammer waiting to snap down on the fence's anvil. The intersection marked a boundary between the city and the county, which for the vehicle's targets meant crossing between bars that close at 1:00 a.m. and those that close at 3:00 a.m. The fences made this intersection into a border crossing where your passport was the color of your skin or the fit of your pants. It was a lot of money for the police to put into a single point, and the streets a few blocks north didn't even have sidewalks.

The Delmar fence made me more aware of all the others. These weren't the Schoemehl pots that the old mayor used for guerilla urbanism, but were rather the county declaring outright warfare on the city. These fences broke up my running routes around Forest Park. A large family of fences broke up DeBaliviere, the avenues around St. Louis University, and countless other north-south roads in order to make driving difficult and bussing nearly impossible. A young puppy of a fence, with big feet and a sense of entitlement, prohibited gathering on a lone non-commercial space on the Delmar Loop, making it impossible to sit down anywhere on "One of the Ten Great Streets in America" without having to buy a beer or an ice cream cone. There is no great street without the array of fences blocking off people who may be interested in arriving from their less-great addresses.

St. Louis is both a wonderful city and one deeply uncomfortable with itself, dividing and conquering its own body like a hateful amoeba. The mix of midwestern stalwartness and southern hospitality that defines St. Louis make for a warm bath of humanity, and the buildings creeping up and out of the Mississippi show all of the wonderful and fascinating things that can be done with red brick. But at the same time, it is a city bluntly founded on defining separateness, famously the spot where Dred Scott was ruled to be human property and less famously the spot where whites lost their "right" to keep non-white families out of their neighborhoods.

This is a city of growth and evacuation and regrowth, and St. Louis is really and truly alive, both in the Jane Jacobs sense of "eyes on the street" and in the biological cell growth-and-decay sense. The decisions that make St. Louis what it is today are at times political and at times haphazard, and the seven-foot fences put these decisions in the ground, codified in black iron.

A fence, in its most literal sense, keeps people out of where they are not wanted. So what is that particular fence doing behind the subjects of Curtis's photograph? It keeps dreadlocked people on the sidewalks and off of the property, not precisely in case of the Ferguson unrest, but also just in case that sort of situation arises. Fences generally serve to ratchet up tension. This fence in particular did just that, then kept a man in harm's way when that tension erupted.

People say St. Louis has changed since 2014, but the fences have by and large remained. A city whose politics—past and present—can be seen in the fences it keeps up doesn't just trap its residents, it traps itself.

Poem to the mother of the white boy I killed

CHRISTOPHER ALEX CHABLÉ

It was not very *carnal*
of me to call *la pinche placa*,
ese. Eso no fue nada sino jams
and hood talk. But I knew them,
puro güeritos, backwards hats, dosing
for *la feria* at *la madrugada*.

I swear, I was afraid for she
who screamed and cursed. *Te juro,*
the bottles crashing against the brick
broke into that *carne pueril* where
only bone *la escudó. Te juro,*
if a *placa* were not to pull up,
I swear, he would have killed her.

I lie to myself, because the babe
durmió, and then *justifiqué* a call
to the executioner, *te juro* I just
thought he'd roll by, and yell,
que apaguen the tunes, yell *son
las cuatro de la madrugada,*

because it was four in the morning.
And the cursing became screams
muffled into something *entre llantos
y carcajadas. Y yo soñoliento,* and I
agotado, ensueñado por four in
the morning. No, I never *haber creido*

la placa would plug one of those
private school kids. *No quiero*

que me hayan aliviado the black
and the blue, and the red lights
in the ally staining like a gorging.
I did not see the body, *no lo quise ver.*

The flashes, steady *rítmicamente*
siguen y disimulo yo que la cinta
flapping its *amarilliente* sheen
inciting caution, inciting caution
—*te juro solamente*—inciting
caution *que es para que arregluen*
algo en la avenida's back alley,

that the *grasa*'s not the grease of greased.
It was not very *carnal* of me
to call on the *chapa* to only
enchapar an hour of sleep
more *que me resultó*
en quemaduras de la soul.

Inside Out

KIERSTAN CARTER

It is April 19, 2015. I am sitting with my back to the engine wall of the Route Sixteen (City Limits) bus, and I am trying to remember all that I've seen of St. Louis.

I have driven lacerations across the city at all hours of the night. I have perched myself under the thin, high-noon shadow of the Gateway Arch. I have eaten at every trendy micro-pasta-taca-indoria to open in the last eighteen months. I have spent whole afternoons on Art Hill. I have cheered for the Cardinals well into October. I have pedaled and sweated down to Tower Grove Park through thick August air. I have lived here through blistering winters and bloody summers. I have learned to take Big Bend to avoid traffic on Skinker. I have memorized all the streets connecting I-64 and I-44 from the county line to the river. I have poured over maps, tracing Olive or Delmar out into the western suburbs. I have lost and found myself in Benton Park, Tower Grove Southeast, the Central West End. And I have traveled where the MetroLink refuses to.

I have spent time getting to know St. Louis, inside and out. I have memorized the grid of its streets and the twisting hills of its suburbs. I have laughed with this city, cried with this city, come to anticipate the sparse skyline when I come home to this city. I have met St. Louis many, many times since first landing in Lambert Airport in 2011. And even though the Sixteen runs the corridor of St. Louis most familiar to me, I can't find a single experience with which to compare this.

Several Sunday nights ago, I visited Publico on the Delmar Loop with Julie. A native St. Louisan, and one of the many assigned to the careful tutelage of students like myself, Julie *loooooves* Publico (emphasis hers). Decorated with the aesthetic cacophony of industrial Central American flare, the "Mexican gastropub"—*Sauce Magazine*'s words, not mine—bustles with springtime foot traffic. Families, couples, friends meeting for drinks huddle in booths, at the bar, around tables. This close to campus, it's rare to find a restaurant where the majority of customers are above the age of twenty-four. Publico, just opened, stands as one of the few places on the Loop yet to be overrun by Wash U. students.

"Overrun" might seem like a harsh description, but I'm bitter. Most days, I would rather not be associated with the groups of late adolescents crowding predictable haunts. Three Kings, Ben and Jerry's, Chipotle have become the commercial extensions of our campus because the Delmar Loop, as it stands now, caters heavily to Wash U. Like every student in the institution's recent history, from the period when it began investing considerable time and energy in establishing itself on a national and global scale, I have experienced St. Louis through the prism of my school's affluence. With every dollar we spend in St. Louis (and on the Delmar Loop specifically), our collective thumbprint presses harder, leaves deeper ridges. The Loop is ours. You feel our dominance on warm weekend afternoons when we spill out of every storefront. It's in the sleepy silence hovering along the corridor of shops and restaurants on weekday mornings. It's the air that prickles with police annoyance at the crowd watching break-dancers at the Chuck Berry statue. Little by little, we are taking over.

Because it'd been on my mind, I asked Julie, "Do you think St. Louis is a foodie town?"

"I think it wants to be." She considers a moment longer, then adds, "but I will say that all of the people I know in St. Louis who go to restaurants as a hobby aren't from here." I perk up at the way she draws out the phrase "from here," because I think I'm from St. Louis. I often feel like I've earned the right to claim St. Louis because my college years, that amorphous phase of nascent adulthood, can be pinned here. But when Julie talks about people that are *from* St. Louis, she isn't talking about me. She's referring to the people she grew up with, went to high school with, who live less than five miles from the houses they grew up in. The kind of people that invest in Blues jerseys and can't understand why anyone would really want to leave. And with her comment about who can or cannot consider themselves from St. Louis, Julie presses on a difference that plays out in a million ways in the region. We talk about St. Louis in terms of divides.

Read any article about the city and you're almost sure to find some reference to the contrast between the "impoverished city proper" with the "affluent western suburbs." A quick Google search returns a number of documentaries, articles, events all focused on "the Delmar Divide." As a region, we're obsessed with our own fragmentation. There is St. Louis and then there's *St. Louis*. There are people that live here and there are people that are from here. I don't mean to suggest that these differences aren't real. One needs only to look at aerial views of the region to see how quickly the landscape changes when you move east to west, and north to south.

But they aren't the only way to understand St. Louis, which is why I'm on this bus.

There are over ninety municipalities dotting St. Louis County, and the Route Sixteen bus route touches the innermost ring of those towns. Beginning in the southern suburb of Shrewsbury, the Route Sixteen bus cuts a path along the city's western limit. I watch Shrewsbury melt into Maplewood, Richmond Height, and Clayton, feel it pull further north into University City, before dipping back in St. Louis briefly. Nestled against the clamoring of the bus's engine, I slide along with the bus through manicured suburban neighborhoods. I began riding buses in 2013, during my first summer in college. Without central air conditioning or much to do in the evenings, Metrobus provided a climate-controlled alternative to watching Netflix in my third story walk-up. At the time I mostly rode the Two Bus (Red) because it stopped outside of my apartment and went to two different grocery stores. But in my leisure time, I learned the Two's route by heart until I could race it on my bike to its major stops at Wash U., in Maplewood, and in Kirkwood—and win. It was through those windows and largely unsolicited conversations with other passengers that I learned how some St. Louisans thought about the city/county difference, and on which side of that line my affiliation with Wash U. placed me.

As we crawl through thick Saturday afternoon traffic, I catch sight of the Loop, dense with pedestrians as it only is in summer. Busy under a plume of dust and activity, the nostalgia of the Delmar Loop cannot be ignored. The Loop reaches back to an earlier period of the city's success. From Blueberry Hill to the trolley line under construction connecting it to Forrest Park, the Loop is full of opportunities to remember St. Louis's history of leisurely grandeur. But as soon as we turn east, we enter a version of urbanity rejected by the Loop's bright lights and memories. The emptier eastern side of the Delmar lacks the luxury of functionality to wrap form around. Vacancy begins to dot the sidewalk and the throng of pedestrians thins so that just a block or two west of the city limit, Delmar seems empty.

The bus stops at the corner of Hamilton and Clemens. One man boards. No one looks.

For the most part, we remain seated, each silent and engrossed in our own worlds as the bus lurches along Hamilton and into the northern half of the city. Plunging into Wellston with a right turn onto Kienlen, the bus route takes us well within the territory of Black St. Louis. Perhaps St. Louis's obsession with divides is couched somewhere in our realities of racial and socioeconomic segregation. With only a few exceptions, we talk about Black St. Louisans, urban poverty, and blight as one, giant, interrelated, geographically-bound problem. Unlike the whiter southern suburbs where the Sixteen's trip began, we're in the part of St. Louis pitied by documentaries and the nightly news.

I wish I could have been here before entire blocks along MLK were razed and replaced with empty plots of land collecting wind-swept trash. I wish I could have been here when Wellston Loop bustled with the kind of traffic that chokes Delmar Loop now. When the pawn shop, a laundromat that's open until 3:00 a.m., and a beauty supply store didn't jut out against the landscape, dusty and gated.

The bus chugs through sections of St. Louis where Black bodies milling about on the streets aren't viewed as evidence of vibrancy or life, but as signs of unemployment and lethargy. As a student transplanted from the East Coast, I've been told in a million different ways that this isn't my St. Louis. I've been given the message that my St. Louis can be found along I-64 moving east to west. My St. Louis doesn't include anything north of Cass Avenue or south of Manchester, and it certainly doesn't include most of the route of the Sixteen Bus. Just a mile north of Delmar, Wellston has all the trappings of a "blighted neighborhood." Boarded-up shops, a building yawning from the missing bricks on its western wall, slumped-in roofs and glass windows caked with dust—it's all there. We treat areas like Wellston and bordering neighborhoods in St. Louis like a scar. They are what remained when post-World War II and post-industrial white flight carried more than half of St. Louis's residents out of the city and into the county. Wellston is part of the St. Louis we're trying to forget. The cinema screen of the bus's windows offers another St. Louis supposedly far removed from my life at Wash U., complete with all the expected tropes about race and class sliding past us.

And onward—north, north, northern still.

The overpowering smell of fried fish pulls my attention beyond the universe of the bus and I begin to watch streets flick by. It's so much greener here than you might expect. Huge trees grow just beyond the road, ripping up the thin excuses for a sidewalk along Kienlen. Wellston becomes Hillsdale and Hillsdale becomes Pine Lawn and every five hundred feet, it feels like one municipality rushes up against the border of another. Every time we crest a new hill on what is now Jennings Station, it seems we exchange one blip of a city for another. It's then—when everything seems to be changing—that I notice, for the first time, a little green sign strapped to a lamppost reading, "End of St. Louis County Maintenance." They're on almost every corner along the bus route, telling you exactly where St. Louis County ends and the City of St. Louis begins. The boundaries between county municipalities come and go, with only a single post announcing the geographic blur of each new town. But there's a brigade of signs to announce the end of the county's responsibility stationed at every possible turn.

Their metallic legality feels like overkill. There's something darkly anxious about our insistence on drawing hard lines between the city and county. The way they won't allow for ambiguity.

When we finally reach Riverview and Hall Metrobus Center, I have to wonder who thought this corner would be a good terminal for so many buses. Less than a mile from the river, at the northernmost point of the city, the Metrobus Center is basically a large parking lot. There's a decaying strip mall across the street, but otherwise we seem to be in an old industrial zone. There are no pedestrians, only cars zooming down Riverview Blvd. In fact, the only part of the scene at Riverview and Hall that matches the views from Shrewsbury, University City, or Wellston, are the green signs hovering at eye level to tell you where the County begins.

If it weren't for the block M on a blue background of the Metro Logo, I might not even recognize this bus station as related to my adventures feverishly pedaling through the Central West End in a race against the One. If it weren't for the green sign militia strapped to every streetlight, I might not notice how the long stretch of rented chain link across from the bus center resembles the iron gates I walk past on my way to class. And if it weren't for this bus ride, I might not see all that St. Louis is trying to pretend that it is not. The longer I live in St. Louis the more I begin to suspect we're all avoiding something, and these signs are just another way to avoid that unnamable thing. We've all suffered a trauma we can't forget—can't live with—and so instead we insist on demarcation, on delineation, on difference.

And in an attempt to move on, we build trolleys. We elect leaders that promise to bring jobs back to downtown. We build our economy around the health care industry. We make strategic five-year development plans. We renovate the Western Expansion museum. We raze old stadiums to make way for new ones. We try to attract corporations. We install bike lanes and encourage farmers' markets. We dig a corridor for a MetroLink to connect eastern and western suburbs. We update brochures and launch a marketing campaign. We start a magazine dedicated to city happenings. We cling to the success of our annual festivals and shows. We make them traditions. We try to pour money and concrete in the empty space left by the hundreds of thousands of people that have left in the last half-century.

We try to nurture a city we can love.

The Sixteen Bus is unlike anything that I've seen in St. Louis because it connects parts of the city that were made for me to the parts of St. Louis that weren't. I know the St. Louis meant to dazzle and welcome. I've learned a version of St. Louis meant for the young, the upwardly mobile, the likely to leave. I'm a citizen of the St. Louis that replaced most of what remains east of Skinker and north of Delmar. I am part of the city that tries to ignore and forget reminders of the traumas of white flight, deindustrialization, urban renewal.

We (I'll include myself among the guilty party one final time) get away with the shorthand of division. We believe the myth of fragmentation because it excuses us from having to know anything else. We let whole parts of St. Louis fall from our minds because it's easier than holding them in tension with our realities.

And so, it is April 19 and I'm riding the Sixteen Bus without any destination in mind because I want to see all of St. Louis and bring my reality into radical convergence with worlds that weren't meant for me. I am trying to remember all that I have seen of St. Louis and I've got a long way to go.

Delmar Loop Pantoum

jason vasser-elong

Never a good sign,
folks pointing, looking around
a mob forms, cars slow
they stop.

Folks pointing looking around
i leave the café to watch,
they stop.
looking at them like the others,

i leave the café to watch
among the rest of us,
and look at them like the others
other poets, artists, the Avant-garde.

Among the rest of us
in tune, inspired
other poets, artists, the Avant-garde
all of us are aware,

inspired
by all the colors,
other poets, artists, the Avant-garde,
we all desire

in tune, we are inspired
admiring the likeness of Chuck Berry
desiring,
man on the corner panhandles.

We admire the likeness of Chuck Berry,
a mob forms, cars slow
man on the corner panhandles
never a good sign.

Downtown St. Louis

ALICE AZURE

After the poetry reading,
I hurry outside, scan traffic
for the yellow of my scheduled taxi ride.

Olive and North Ninth Streets
bustle with customers rushing
to beat the culinaria's closing time.
With bulging white plastic bags
wrapped around their wrists
they head for their cars or into the night—
past the panhandler begging for money.

Skull cap rolled low on her forehead,
short gray coat flapping with the wind—
she scuffs back and forth in skimpy brown slippers,
asking—over and over—for any spare change.

Soon the neon lights start to flicker out.
Pursing her lips, she shuffles to where I stand.
My shoulders dig deeper into the wall.
Her arms swing back and forth,
end with a clap and a rasping, *Got any change?*
No, I say and look away.
She continues her swinging vigil.
When a cab drives by
I wave wildly, run to the street—
mindless of the forty-dollar fare
to my suburban home.

Sk8 Sanctuary

KAITLYN HOUGH

"Be careful, and try to follow my steps."

Rebekah Jarchow expertly climbs the partially rotten wooden stair-case to what was once a choir loft. Balancing on the edges of some steps and completely avoiding those warped with rot, the willowy blonde leads me to the second level of Saint Liborius. The loft, though coated with a thick layer of dust and pigeon feathers, boasts an impressive view of the expansive ground floor of the church. Though it is the modern renovations that immediately draw the eye, the scars of a 162-year history make themselves present in the form of drywall cracks and amorphous water damage stains in the scarce wall space untouched by graffiti.

From the outside, Saint Liborius Catholic Church appears to be collateral damage, one of many buildings fallen victim to the rapid deterioration of North St. Louis. Tucked into the historic St. Louis Place neighborhood at Hogan Street and North Market Street, its immense, red brick facade stretches upward into a prominent bell tower and looms over the surrounding buildings, despite having lost its spire in the 1960s. Torn screens and shattered stained glass windows give onlookers the impression of a worn, weary building, weighed down by the memories of the countless congregations and clergies from its past. To a passerby, Saint Liborius gives no indication that behind its massive red doors exists one of the most compelling resurrection stories this city has seen. "Skaters get shit done, and they're really the only ones that could take on this process," Jarchow says.

Within the nave of the church, the benches, which once seated the neighborhood's parishioners, have been replaced with wooden ramps. The ramps sprawl across the floor of the church to the bema, where the altar once stood. The vaulted ceilings now reverberate with the satisfying scrape of skateboard wheels meeting wood—a new hymn for a new congregation. Formerly white walls now drown in color, as graffiti style murals mingle with the building's original Catholic frescoes. This is Sk8 Liborius, where skateboarding is the religion and skaters and artists have become the clergy.

Established in 1856, Saint Liborius Catholic Church served as the local parish for the large population of German Catholics who had come to reside in the northern end of St. Louis. Designed in Gothic Revival style by German American architect William Schickel, the grand church was built with the anticipation of a growing parish. However, despite a century of activity following the building's completion in 1889, Saint Liborius's parish began to diminish as more and more Catholics moved west to the suburbs—following a pattern of white flight that forever changed parts of St. Louis—taking their need for a large Catholic church with them. In 1992, Saint Liborius closed its doors and auctioned its interior furnishings. The church would remain closed and unmaintained until 2012 when it was purchased by local skater Forest Mattli.

Despairing at the idea of allowing the distinguished building to continue to sit unused, or to be demolished for corporate redevelopment, Mattli called on a group of friends, including skaters David Blum, John Dudrey, and Bryan Bedwell, to help rehabilitate the abandoned church. Having been neglected for nearly twenty years, Saint Liborius's state of disrepair has proven to be a colossal undertaking for the group. The kaleidoscopic stained glass windows, once tall and gleaming, have lost several panes to weather damage and alleged theft by a phony real estate agent. These missing panes served as an alternate entry to the church for the likes of rain, hail, rodents, and countless pigeons, whose carcasses and feces had come to litter the once carpeted floor. The dark, damp building has become the ideal growing environment for mold, and abandoned pieces of woodwork have begun to rot. Within the first year of rehabilitation alone, no fewer than five rollaway dumpsters were required to dispose of damaged and hazardous materials from within the church. Even as the rebuilding process has commenced, building cleanup continues to be a work in progress. With limited manpower and funding to complete repairs, the weather-damaged roof and yet to be replaced windowpanes continue to expose the interior of the building to the elements, creating a "two steps forward, one step back" cycle for Sk8 Liborius's founders.

Despite the challenges they face with repairing and rebuilding the church, the group seems to foster no doubt that Sk8 Liborius will reach, if not surpass, its former glory.

Jarchow, Sk8 Liborius's newly appointed art director, is eager to point out rooms and spaces in varying states of construction and indicates their proposed future functions. The staircase from the ground floor to the choir loft continues up to the defunct bell tower, where she suggests a rock climbing course may one day fill the inner walls of the tower. Across the church and tucked behind the bema, another set of (much less precarious) stairs leads to the former sacristy, where priests once prepared for mass. Within the sacristy, thrifted furniture has transformed the room into a studio apartment, complete with a bathroom and kitchenette. "We try to salvage as much of the church's original elements as possible. We pulled this from the basement," Jarchow says, gesturing toward the marble tile surrounding the shower. Heading back to the ground floor, Jarchow explains that the goal is to give every area of the church a distinct function, including the rectory, which will eventually be adapted into classrooms and art studios.

Though funding is at the forefront of obstacles facing projects like these, it often proves to be the tip of the proverbial iceberg. For a century-old building to become legally functional for modern use, there are numerous modifications required to get up to current building codes. Lead pipes, such as those lingering behind the walls of Saint Liborius, need to be replaced, and modern fire codes must be adhered to. Unfortunately, these modifications often require various permits and inspections, which can become time-consuming and costly to acquire. "Right now, we're kind of flying under the radar," Jarchow admitted during my first visit there in 2017, perched on the top edge of one of the ramps. For those involved with the project, it makes more sense to begin building and working toward achieving a passable status in terms of building codes before bringing an inspector in, rather than waiting to obtain the necessary permits to advance the project. The risk here lies in the potential fines to be issued for work without permits, as well as liability costs should anyone be harmed in an uninspected, uninsured building. Though Sk8 Liborius is certainly working toward achieving properly inspected, functional status, as Dudrey puts it, "On the north side, too, they have bigger fish to fry."

Indeed, North St. Louis is not lacking for problems. Still suffering the effects of mid-twentieth-century white flight, which, incidentally, is a probable cause for the ultimate closing of Saint Liborius, North St. Louis has consistently struggled with crime and poverty. In an attempt to bring jobs and revitalize the ailing sector of St. Louis, developer Paul McKee pitched St. Louis as a destination for the relocation of the National Geospatial-Intelligence Agency. The decision for the NGA to build its western headquarters in St. Louis was finalized on June 2, 2016, to the excitement of city officials, and to the dismay of many North St. Louis residents fearing the seizure of their family homes. In an attempt to either save face, or to genuinely improve the community surrounding the agency's new location (one can never be completely sure), NGA officials have been looking into design concepts which will allow for interaction and development in the community, rather than solely focusing on building the campus. For Sk8 Liborius, this has led to a dialogue with NGA developers, which has proven to provide valuable advice and connections in its growth. For skaters and artists with limited experience in grant writing and developing, the NGA has become an unexpected ally in the quest to achieve full operations.

Part of Sk8 Liborius's goal as a community center is to help prevent the potential gentrification as a result of the NGA's presence in North St. Louis. Though the NGA's relocation has the potential to foster a beneficial spike in the economy and job market of the surrounding area, a primary concern is whether these benefits will apply to the current, largely impoverished, mostly black residents, or if they will simply attract upper middle-class workers and push the current inhabitants aside. With the population of North St. Louis having been continuously overlooked for years, gentrification is a very real fear for those who live and work in the area, and it is something that Sk8 Liborius has at least tried to keep in mind as it moves forward in its plans for the future. "We want to help *ease* gentrification," Jarchow notes. "We want to be a good thing for this community."

Though Sk8 Liborius aims to open an inclusive community center, there are also specific plans in place to be active in the community, particularly when it comes to the local youth. With the immediate attraction of a skate park, Sk8 Liborius has the potential to serve as a safe space for local kids to stimulate creativity that is often neglected within the public school systems.

For all its good intentions, however, Sk8 Liborius is faced with its critics. Due to the aforementioned "under the radar" status, knowledge of Sk8 Liborius in the greater St. Louis area is fairly limited (though, somehow word managed to reach rapper Lil Wayne, who dropped by in 2016). However, those within the immediate vicinity have had little to no problems with its developments. Since its purchase in 2012, Sk8 Liborius has received only three police referrals from surrounding neighbors. For the most part, criticism has mostly come from those who view the adaptation of a former place of worship as sacrilegious, or who do not understand its greater mission. One such criticism comes from art scholar Eugene D. Markowski, who claimed in a response to a local architecture blog post that, "To turn Saint Liborius Church into a recreation center is in itself an obscene act of vandalism. . . . I would rather see the church demolished rather than turned into something it was never intended to be."

Perhaps the most substantial nod to the building's past, however, lies within the group's passion for service. At the end of the day, Sk8 Liborius is, as Jarchow puts it, "not just skaters throwing parties." In fact, the goals for outreach programs through Sk8 Liborius closely mirror those of local Catholic churches. The group dreams of establishing a mentorship program, in which teenagers and young adults of various ages would be matched with a mentor within Sk8 Liborius who would then work to teach his or her mentee a trade or skill. "They could come and work in exchange for an art or skate class," Jarchow explains. "We want to teach that you work as is necessary, not just when you want to."

Sk8 Liborius may no longer be a church in a traditional sense, with worship now taking the form of skating, and an adapted gospel being taught through the graffiti on the walls, but it is trying to become a sanctuary for those who have been overlooked in St. Louis. As Jarchow puts it, "It's a community. It's a family that believes in something bigger, so we work together to make it happen."

Saturday Afternoon Train on Game Day

MARÍA BALOGH

Scenes pass by the window
the train in motion through
the city, parks, smoking factories,
condos, brown downtown buildings,
billboards, billboards, billboards,
fast food franchise, fast food franchise

Public transport, city USA
people in and out
many oblivious to the
commotion around them

Boys serious as men,
riding with their fathers

Tomorrow is Fathers' Day
a man reminds his fellow
riders, getting cheers from
the crowds in red outfits
He stands at the front of the car,
despite the availability of seats

Men playful as boys, teasing,
punching each other, between
them two women, one pregnant,
feeling her swollen belly through
a red jersey every few seconds
as if to reconfirm
seemingly unafraid
of being in the crossfire
of the men's playful punches

Red caps, red sweats, red pants,
red bandanas, red T-shirts,
children, women, men, old, young—
same destination, all

The train almost empties
at Busch Stadium

The all-American beloved
ball game consumes this
Saturday afternoon
in the city's railways

St. Louis takes a break today,
in support of her Cardinals.

～

Entering Illinois
the scene outside transforms:
rusty turf equipment, Bobcats,
farmhouses, fields of crops,
heavy machinery, dense vegetation,
stagnant flood waters, visible tadpoles,
subdivisions of houses in the same patterns,
same colors, same materials

Are the people living there also so invariable?

A hearse races alongside
the train lifting dust
from the gravel rural road,
giving a feeling of dryness
in the middle of wetness

Ten stations to reach the last stop
in Illinois—a woman gives
her party a wake-up call
to arrange for a pick up

of her and her duffle bag
before dozing off again,
her hair extremely short,
a look of tiredness

A soldier coming home?

~

The train reverses direction
to return toward Missouri,
back to the city
A woman alone, dressed in red,
four old men also in red,
board the westbound train

Below the bridge, the river
threatens to invade the buildings
and parking lots at its borders,
everyone hoping that 2008
does not become a great
deluge, like that of '93

The Gateway to the West
offers its majestic curves
overlooking the casinos
filled with tourists,
perhaps a local or two

Past the stadium's station once again,
the riders fewer and fewer,
as the afternoon fades into evening
before the end of the game

Did we win or lose this day?
I don't know, I guard my notes
and go sit on the grass
of U. City Public Library
and share them
with my fellow writers

variations on a suburb

MEGAN STRINGER

the largest catsup bottle in the world is just full of water—
a trademarked tower standing bright red in Collinsville, Illinois.
a novelist on a magazine assignment drove by one day,
writing "Brooks' Original" in American Rural Red,
photographer painting the bottle like a cold glass of coke in a diner.
but the duo forgot to note the face my dad would make walking by as a kid,
trudging away from his fussy older sister, looking for
adventure (a way out) in roadside attractions. Catholic parents growing old,
the kids would find their freedom eventually: Aunt Cathy in an overlarge
humid state on the border, Houston highways suffocating the child she
didn't have;
Uncle John in a frigid rectangle state up north, Omaha breathing in
boarding schools and zoos for after-school fun; my dad, just over
the Mississippi outside St. Louis, driving in and out of the city—
a reminder we stay the same except for the suburb we choose to raise kids in.

Secret Socialist Lover

PAMELA GARVEY

Our final embrace: my cheek against his chest while a child's shoes smacked the sidewalk behind us. Back and forth she ran, despite St. Louis heat. Eyes closed, as if that might cloud over the inevitable, I held on tight. It was one of those rare moments when I could feel the earth spinning beneath me.

Two years before in 2015, when he contacted me on OkCupid, I hesitated: he a labor lawyer representing management, and I, a card-carrying union member. But he had that olive skin and those dark eyes. And damn he was smart. We conversed online about Foucault's Pendulum, a physics experiment that astonishes both of us. So not just smart, but intellectual.

He lives in University City. I didn't question why a divorced man with a grown child had just purchased a 3,000 square foot home. Or that I only saw white people on his block. After all, from his house, we could stroll to the Loop. And, as he frequently pointed out, he had all kinds of friends.

I wouldn't know because I never met them. I asked to spend time with his friends. He said, of course. But it never happened. I thought, *he's so busy working seventy hours a week, he wants the little time we have just for us.* But in brief flashes of insight: *because he devotes seventy hours a week to crushing unions, he needs me compartmentalized: a photo to show, lover stored in the wallet like papers proving insurance.*

Maybe one poker night, he pulled out my photos. Maybe one of the guys incited jealousy by commenting on my long legs. Or maybe they noted his preference for women with an Irish complexion and blue eyes, then warned him to stay away from his "type."

Or maybe he simply constructs his life like a hive, each comb its own compartment, separate from the others. Which was I? Secret socialist lover? Too sticky to ever meet friends or daughter?

My life is more like Foucault's Pendulum. Rather than the sequestered world of the hive, I dangle in the open. After a year together, he'd socialized with many of my loved ones. Yet I still had not met one of his friends.

Pendulums seem to sway aimlessly. But nothing about Foucault's Pendulum is aimless. It's the certainty of gravity. Despite appearances, it's not even a sway; it's a slow, almost imperceptible pivot pulling me clockwise into a future of my own. I began to recede. I refused to accept his visit or his offer to run my errands during a post-op convalescence. He sent a book of maps with an inscription about me as the path he'd finally found. The first map in the book was entitled "False Map of True North." It was an atlas of geographic misconceptions.

After I healed from surgery, we dated again. It was like trying to love the sun; how could I touch something so far away?

Maybe when he offered to pay for my dog's surgery, he hoped it'd secure his place at the center while I orbited in the distance he lit with dollar bills.

I wanted to scream, "fuck your money." I politely said no. I still quivered as his fingers slid along my hip. Hungry for his touch, I'd fight back the urge to slap his face.

When he gave me jewelry, scarves, and books I didn't want, I said thank you. Who did he grill in the courtroom for money to purchase those gifts? Did he donate to the Right to Work candidate for governor? Who was this man who said Obama was extreme because of how the Justice Department handled Ferguson? Was he saying this shit the year before? Were he and his friends desperate to win their country back from the black man? Was I spinning so much I couldn't hear him straight?

Underneath his body, I felt as if my skin unzipped. I could never keep my eyes open when I came. Would've been like staring straight into high noon.

I confess: I miss the snippets of Neruda he'd text me. I miss the evenings we cooked in his kitchen, naked, putting olives in each other's mouths. I miss the conversations we had about how awful Trump is. How I texted him from an airport to let him know that Trump eats steak well-done—a travesty, we both agreed. In the primaries, I voted for Bernie and he for Kasich (or so he said). He defined himself as a moderate.

Moderates don't donate money to the Ferguson police officers.

By now, Ferguson has become an emblem of institutional racism. Many don't know Ferguson is a microcosm not only of racism in the US, but also of St. Louis itself—one of the most segregated cities in the nation. One of the sharpest divisions in the country is Delmar Boulevard, near where my former lover lives. On the south side are million dollar mansions owned mostly by whites. On the north side, an impoverished community of almost entirely black Americans. Separated by two car lengths, yet they are as far apart as the poles. North of Delmar are food deserts, abandoned buildings, gangs, and whole communities disproportionately representing the 26 percent of the city that struggles with hunger. Whether compiling data on crime, poverty, or the lowest life spans, the portrait of St. Louis as a whole is skewed because North City and North County tilt the scales so heavily.

How could the riots in Ferguson surprise anyone who lived in St. Louis? How could anyone who understood Foucault's Pendulum not wince at the irony of living in the city of the famous Dred Scott case? One hundred sixty years after that trial, I wondered if the city had progressed much more than the earth does in its rotation. He, of course, disagreed. When I told him about white men in a truck running a black friend off the road days after the election, he told me she should've called the police with their license plate number. She's trying to steer herself to safety and she's supposed to memorize their license plate? Not to mention this incident happened in Ferguson. There's no way she'd feel comfortable trusting the Ferguson police.

He believes justice prevails. I believe privilege prevails. He quickly pointed out that I live in Tower Grove South, the most left-leaning voting district in the state of Missouri and one of the only neighborhoods besides Ferguson where people took to the streets to proclaim Black Lives Matter; if that wasn't far left enough for me, had I considered another country? Our homes less than ten miles apart, no one could ever map how far apart we really lived.

After our break up, I changed my dating profile to read, "If you voted for Trump or Greitens, don't contact me."

When we broke up, he said, "Let's face it: in the revolution we're on opposite sides."

Only halfway through its prime, the sun won't change for another five billion years, at which point its core will begin to shrink. Maybe that accounts for his talk about all empires ending, about how everything is miniscule in the grand scheme of things. In the galaxy, there is no true north. Maybe that's why he needs others orbiting around him. Maybe when he put his hand on my throat during sex, he was thinking of my leftist politics. Of the impending solar eclipse.

Humans of St. Louis

LINDY DREW

"I remember when I found out I was having a boy. At the ultrasound, I shed a tear because I thought, 'Oh my god, I'm going to raise a Black man. How do I keep him alive? How do I keep him on the path?' Black boys just don't get the benefit of the doubt, they're clearly targeted, and the idea of justice being served for them is really gray. It was four years ago when I was looking at the ultrasound. The tear was on one side of my face, and my husband was on the other side. I'm glad he didn't see it because I said, 'Oh, yay!' But, yeah, I felt the weight of the world on my shoulders."

"I like pancakes!"

"We lived in Nepal for eighteen years as refugees from Bhutan. We didn't have IDs, green cards, resident cards, or citizenship there. We never saw the dream of living in the United States. Now, I've been in St. Louis for one and a half years. We learned British English in our country."

"What's your favorite word in English?"

"Awesome. So I nicknamed my two-year-old baby Awesome."

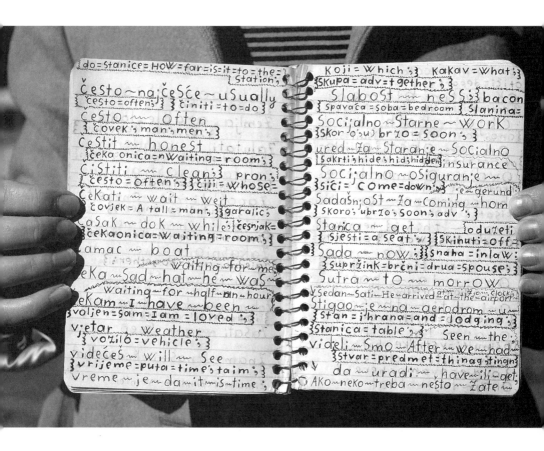

"After my grandpa, Saifija Selimagic, passed away, my mom was going through all of his stuff and there's a few dozen of these notebooks of him trying his best to learn English in his seventies. He was obsessed with learning. If he heard a new word, like on TV or on the radio, he would write it down. Or, if somebody was around, they would translate it for him. He was born in the same village I was but into abject poverty. My situation wasn't much better, but I had food as a child. My mom tells me about how he would go through the village as a child and find food that people left for animals outside, collect it, and bring it back home for himself and his siblings. It still blows my mind because his personality, his messages, his teachings, everything he did is why I am who I am today. I have this vivid memory of him when we were at my uncle's house and his in-laws were saying racist things about black people, calling them all these names, and saying horrible things. And my grandpa, a sheepherder in the mountains who hadn't met a black person until his fifties—because Bosnia is very white and our village only had like 700 people—raised his hands up with this way of quieting a room. He was so calm and eloquent and said, 'You can't reduce a whole population of people based on a handful of people that you met. That's what was done to us. That's why we're living in a country that isn't ours.' And the way he said it, relating it back to our situation, was so powerful for me in the third grade."

"I've been homeless for almost four months now. A friend of mine gave me a heater for the truck I'm living in right now. I keep myself together, but it's hard to get help. If somebody could support me with clothes and shelter, that would be fine. Money would be fine, but it's not what I'm searching for. Just a decent place to stay, food, and some clothes to wear. Living in a car is not nice. It's hard to sleep. I've got to stay alert because anybody can walk up. It's not like I'm safe. There are accidents right here almost every night. In the morning I have to go somewhere to wash my face and hands. When it's cold, it's cold. And when it's hot, it's hot."

"That's my biological mother and this is my drag mother. That's the week and this is the weekend."

"We share custody. And when she's acting up, then I call her and say, 'Hey, your daughter. . . !'"

"I met her at Denese's Nightclub in East St. Louis. She said she was from Twenty-seventh and Ridge and I said, 'No you're not because I'm from Twenty-seventh and Ridge.' Turned out she knew my whole family but she didn't know me. I moved to Tennessee for a while and came back. My dream was always to find a girl from the neighborhood."

Jaywalking

ADAM STEEVENS

My story begins and ends with the same question: "Can you fix it?"

I worked as a mobile phone technician for Sprint from 2012 to 2015. Over those years, I bounced from store to store, but I spent most of my time in Florissant, swapping out broken touchscreens and busted camera lenses for thousands of customers in North County. The best repairs were the ones that were prefaced with an absurd and unfailingly intricate story. *I know it looks bad, but I was baking, and I had the oven door open, and I tripped and dropped it into a hot oven.* Lucky for her, the phone just needed a new plastic housing to replace the one she had melted. *There's a hole in the floor of my car, and the Blackberry fell into it and I ran it over in my driveway.* Hang on, you're driving around with holes in your floorboard? *My email account stopped working after my house was struck by lightning.* If you'll forgive the pun, how shocking.

Servicing people's phones is an intimate business. Each repair could be an emotional adventure. You might accidentally encounter someone's amateur pornography while troubleshooting their camera, or you might have a tearful widow ask if there is any way you could revive her husband's last voicemails from her device. A client might hand you a phone that had been dunked in their toilet, or they might ask you to troubleshoot an issue with the *secret* memory card taped to the inside of their battery door. We did it all—hazard material handling or marital affair tech support—and I came to learn about the soul of North County one splintered touchscreen at time.

In a perfect world, Ferguson would be as internationally recognizable as Dellwood, Charlack, or Ballwin. Instead, it has become synonymous with the unrelenting ugliness of midwestern racism and police brutality. Michael Brown was killed in Ferguson on August 9, 2014, but the racial animus in and around that community existed long before his death, and will persist long after it, too. The drastic racial and economic divide, between black and white St. Louisans, was plainly reflected in my customers' phones. The white hedge-fund kids bought the latest iPhones, and the pre-paid 'feature' phones often ended up in black and brown hands. Of course, the poverty presented practical problems for the company. A bill payment machine—a popular fixture in a phone store—was once embedded into the side of the building, available at all hours like an ATM. This machine was moved inside after some enterprising criminals tried to yank it out of the wall with a winch.

The gritty realities of poverty had become an aspect of the job. Learning to squash your natural human empathy was part of getting through the workday. Phones are an expensive necessity, and when they couldn't be fixed, less fortunate people had little to no recourse. It wasn't uncommon for customers to cry when you waddled out from the back to break the bad news. A millisecond of clumsiness could cost you hundreds of dollars. The company would stock the most ridiculous and flatly unnecessary products for the sales team to sell; Wi-Fi-connected doorbells, phone screen projection systems, and pool-proof Bluetooth speakers were just some of the superfluous plastic junk these sales reps were expected to push every day. Returns counted against their pay, and the mounds of accessories they sold too often came back after the customer got sticker-shock from the first bill. The pickings were better in Chesterfield and Maryland Heights, they said, because the rich white folks lived out there and had money to burn.

I was working in Florissant in 2012—the year Trayvon Martin was killed by George Zimmerman—and the workplace arguments about the shooting between white and black coworkers were unforgettable. These were not polite disagreements, but literal screaming matches. "Zimmerman won't survive in prison," one African American coworker insisted, "the street has already spoken." To one white, Chesterfieldian co-worker, this suggestion was *even worse* than what Zimmerman did to Martin. They barked and hollered at one another until the store manager told them both to zip it. The racial tension wasn't percolating underground anymore. It was overt, unmistakable, and suffocating.

As a post-collegiate twenty-something, I naturally preferred working a closing shift in those days. One evening, I went to lock up the store with a black co-worker. He reached for the key, and as it tumbled around in the lock, I started to walk back to my car. "Hey, stick around for a second," he asked with a chuckle, "cops driving past might think I'm breaking in if there isn't a white guy standing next to me." I laughed politely but he wasn't really joking, and I wasn't really laughing. The racial inequity, the differences in the classes of our citizenship was incontrovertible, as tangible to us both as the air in our lungs.

With a decade of retail experience under my belt, I was quite used to customer outbursts during my years with Sprint. The *can-I-speak-to-the-manager* pouting sessions are an unavoidable aspect of the service industry.

I was subjected to one such retail tantrum at the hands of a uniformed Florissant police officer. The policeman entered the store, and within a few moments, had recognized one of my supervisors and approached him holding a broken Android phone. They yelled back and forth for a few seconds before my supervisor, who is black, retreated into an employee-only area in the back, visibly perturbed, holding back tears. The cop walked toward the exit, but instead of leaving, he posted up on the door and tucked his hands into his belt. He was, ostensibly, waiting for my co-worker to leave. Willing to wait however long it took to settle their score.

I slipped into the back room and overheard an avalanche of panicked words, stuttered in staccato breaths—"He's arrested me before, he followed me home and yanked me out of my car and pushed me up against my garage door"—and after a couple of timorous questions, I discovered that the officer was upset because his phone screen was shattered and my manager had refused to replace it. This was the standard policy we gave to everyone, one that was plainly codified in the contract every subscriber signed, but the officer wanted it fixed regardless. At the time, one of the few managerial powers that came with my job title was the ability to circumvent the insurance policy for 'discretionary customer satisfaction.' I approached the officer and asked him if he would leave if I fixed the phone free of charge. He handed the device back to me and snorted, "You tell your buddy if he's got a fuckin' problem with me, we can take that shit outside right now."

It was in this moment that my bubble of white ignorance was popped. Growing up, I was never afraid of the police; and I never had a reason to fear them because they never treated me poorly. The reason for this preferential treatment became more and more obvious with every passing second I lived in Florissant. Law enforcement, *by default,* makes life easier for me because of the color of my skin. No one in a uniform had *ever* spoken to me the way he had spoken about my black co-worker. I lived in the same community as my black peers, but make no mistake, I did not live in their universe. They were burdened with a yoke I couldn't begin to understand. By all accounts, the now-infamous altercation between Michael Brown and Darren Wilson first began because Brown was jaywalking, or at the very least, simply not walking on a sidewalk.

Living within eyeshot of my place of employment gave me a rather enviable commute. When the weather was nice, I would walk to work in the space of a couple minutes. This jaunt—from my apartment at Kensington Square on North New Florissant Road to the Sprint store on

Lindbergh—would lead me across Highway 67, one of North County's most congested arteries of traffic. Like Brown, I didn't much care for sticking to the sidewalks. I jaywalked nearly every single day. Often, I jaywalked *multiple* times a day. If I wanted a drink, I'd skip over to the nearby gas station or head to the fast food joint just across the street and promptly walk back when I was done. On several occasions, I jaywalked *in front of moving Florissant police cruisers.* Unlike Brown, I am white. I have never been stopped by the police for jaywalking. I had the privilege of not being grabbed by an officer from a moving vehicle for such an insignificant offense.

White midwesterners have developed an uncanny ability to speak fluently in coded language. As white suburbanites, we know what Grandpa *really* means when he says that he wants us to roll up the windows and lock the doors when we're driving around in the city. We know what our white friends *really* mean when they say they only go downtown for sporting events. This peculiarity intensified after Brown was killed six and a half miles away from the Sprint store. As the riots and unrest started to spread, my mobile phone began to fill with leading questions: *Are you guys doing all right? How far away are you from the riots?*

The protests made corporate fairly antsy. Boost Mobile, a subsidiary of Sprint, had one of its retail locations in Florissant looted during the riots, and management made the decision to shut down our store early one afternoon as a result. Before heading home, we took the phones out of their locked cabinets on the sales floor and moved them into the inventory room in the back in the hopes that only our "demo" phones could be snatched in a smash-and-grab. The looters never materialized, of course, and the devices were placed back in the cabinets the next morning. Sprint was in the community to make money, not to lose it, and the security measures often bordered on the absurd.

We kept millions of dollars in iPhones locked away in a seven-foot-tall gun safe that was bolted to the floor. At first we only stored the Apple inventory in the safe, but the list of items the closing crew was expected to jam into the gun safe grew to include display tablets and even our own laptop workstations. The safety of people always came first, the corporate loss prevention officer told us, because money and property were replaceable and insured for loss. A request for additional lighting in the parking lot after some of the female technicians said they felt unsafe walking back to their cars at night was out of the question, but for the iPhones, a safe that a thief would need an arc-welder to penetrate was completely reasonable.

The white fixation on property became a permanent fixture in the discussions that surrounded the unrest. Conversations among white observers about Ferguson were usually bookended with a condescending screed about how utterly foolish it was for the protesters to be obliterating their own communities. This was the viewpoint from which a large segment of the white Missourian world viewed this movement, conflating most of the peaceful demonstrators with the select few among them who picked up bricks and torched vehicles. After the riots, I caught up with an old acquaintance I went to church with when I was younger. He ended up working for QuikTrip for decades, managing stores all throughout the greater St. Louis region. When I asked about the incinerated QT in Ferguson, he shrugged and said that at this stage, it was "a $30 million insurance claim." Crime is crime at the end of the day, I suppose, but I don't know how anyone felt more empathy for a business losing property than two parents losing their son.

When I think about the people of North County, my mind often drifts back to the time I spent repairing their mobile phones. We would stack them in a lineup when the store got busy, working the repairs in an assembly line. I remember the outlandish phone cases that stood out in the queue, adorned with sparkling glitter and golden sequins or overlaid with fashionable stripes of vivid neon, a favorite team's logo, or the icon of a childhood comic book hero. North County didn't want another lifeless slab of unimaginative grey in their pockets. They wanted the most colorful thing they could get their hands on.

Once powered up, you would commonly see the phone's lock-screen personalized with images of the customer's children, grinning warmly in navy-blue school uniforms with the photographer's watermark still visible. Smartphones are a little jagged chunk of someone's personality, and when a customer entrusts it to you, even for the tiniest repair, you get an unvarnished glimpse of who they are and what they care most about. This was, in retrospect, what made it sting the most when I heard such caustic criticism of the Ferguson protesters, reduced by their detractors to a vicious group of looters and rioters. I encountered the vibrancy of their inimitable humanity on a daily basis and it changed my perspective forever. How could I make the rest of the world see my neighbors the way I saw them? The narrative was poisoned, and I was powerless to change it.

The helplessness I felt underscored a bitter truth, that this community was as broken as a shattered phone screen, and no one could stop talking around the actual problem. The proposed solutions rolled in from the outside world like waves. It was body cameras, or revisions of use-of-force doctrines, or increased use of non-lethal weaponry by police, or anything that would ignore the elephant in the room that no one wanted to call by name.

When a phone first comes to a technician for a repair, the first step in the process is to perform "triage." It is a word the technical world shares with the medical one. Your doctor, your mechanic, and your IT guy all have a strikingly similar triage process. It always begins with a sober appraisal of the condition of the subject and an estimate of the severity of the issue. Fellow white people, we are the cause of the problem. Ferguson erupted because of our white anxiety, because of the boiling racial resentment lying dormant in our bodies, honed to subtle perfection over hundreds of years of white dominion. And tragically, we both know our white demons have an incontrovertible body count that continues to rise. The killing, the riots, the unrest, and the division will stop once we come to grips with the impulses that make our brains believe an unarmed black teenager is a threat by default. It is my whiteness, it is your whiteness, not their blackness, that is broken and in desperate need of repair.

My story begins and ends with the same question: "Can you fix it?"

Uncontrolled Eruptions

ALONZO ADAMS

It was a cold December morning in Ferguson in 1984 or '85—a couple of days after Christmas. I was ten or eleven. My parents had gotten me a BB gun for Christmas that year, a replica of a .22 caliber, pump-action rifle type. My dad grew up in Mississippi and was an avid hunter. The church my father pastored owned some land down the street where my grandmother grew her garden. There were several trees and fields that were host to plenty of small game. I couldn't wait to get outside and find some small game in the trees or in the field.

As I walked slowly down Dade Avenue, pretending to stalk my prey, suddenly two or three police cars pulled up around me. The police drew their guns and told me to get on the ground. Terrified, I told them I wanted to go home and get my mother.

"I said get on the ground and throw your hands up," one of them answered, yelling.

As I look back on the shooting of Tamir Rice—a twelve-year-old black boy with a BB gun, who was shot dead by police in 2014—I realize I am blessed to still be able to tell this story.

Somehow—through the fear you can imagine how a young boy would feel with real guns pointed at him—I complied. The police took my BB gun. When they realized it was a toy, they released me and allowed me to go home, but told me it was dangerous to walk up and down the street with a gun. Looking back on my walk home that cold morning, I now see that moment was my introduction to a harsh reality. That would not be the last time I would be engaged by the police for something I was carrying that threatened them: the color of my skin.

Growing up, I witnessed similar incidents playing out on Dade Avenue, where my home and church were located. My parents, older sister, and younger brother saw many car chases (two that led to the cars driving into the basement of the church), and even the killing of a young black man by the police in front of our home.

It was late evening like any other on our street. I can't remember the date or even the year. The only thing that I can remember was it was dark, and before it was over, there was a dead black man lying close to us in the alley across the street. I was afraid, and aside from a funeral, I had never seen a dead man's body before. I remember Daddy telling me to go in the house and not to watch. I remember him talking to the detective and telling them he saw the police throw a gun over where the body was laying, but it was never put into the report as far as I know.

Incidents like these are frequently talked about among the African American community, from Rodney King to Tamir Rice to Michael Brown. Michael Brown was an unarmed teenager shot and killed by a white Ferguson police officer on August 9, 2014, just a few miles from where the police had pointed guns at me thirty years before.

It was a casualty that became a catalyst, opening a crack that would allow years of tension to explode.

Not only am I the pastor of our church, but I am also a musician. The day Michael was killed, one of my musician cousins (most of us are musically inclined) from Denver was here, and we were having a jam session at the church when we heard that another young black teen was killed by a white cop. Sadly, we didn't pay it all the attention it deserved. It wasn't that uncommon, and if we really thought the whole process through, we would just get angry. The usual chain of events would go something like this: white cop kills black man, then white cop would get placed on administrative leave while the police chief announced there would be a "fair and transparent investigation" by an "independent, outside agency." The officer would say the key phrase—he feared for his life and the safety of his partner. There would be no charges, and black folks would just have to be mad and suck it up. Yeah, that about sums it up.

I didn't want to add fuel to the fire. There were already riots, vandalisms, attacks on the police, and many other things that were destroying the neighborhoods where the majority of the blacks lived and worked. It was said that we destroyed our own neighborhoods, but in retrospect, we knew if we did go to the neighborhoods of the affluent, this whole fiasco would have taken a new twist.

The black male victims continue to pile up like bodies in the morgues and graveyards, but the police officers are being placed on what mostly appears to be a paid vacation (called "paid administrative leave") for the slaughter of people who look just like me.

Are we angry? Do we feel unheard, like we have been pushed to the side? Do the studies and real-life experiences prove that we have been unfairly targeted but have been given less than most of the other oppressed people? Absolutely. The police officers are still able to kill black men and not face justice.

Why aren't the officers booked and paraded around and humiliated? Is all life sacred? Is my life worth as much as a police officer's? Why would I get life in prison or the death penalty for killing an officer, but he or she would get one month off with pay for killing me?

As much as I was hurt and disappointed by the looting and destruction of property in the days following Michael Brown's death, the only thing that seems to get attention by the media is blood, bullets, and chaos. No one would have given Ferguson a second look had it not been for the "unrest."

So who will tell our story? None of this is anything new. Thanks to social media, we are able to spread our own news and allow America to see it—but it hasn't changed anything. We are still dying at the hands of white officers, even with the mandate of body cams, even as there are more cameras in the world than ever before. Why would you think proof of video would make a difference now, when it didn't March 3, 1991, when the world watched four police officers beat Rodney King?

The rage seen in Ferguson after Michael Brown's death wasn't new. His fateful encounter with officer Darren Wilson simply was the straw that broke the camel's back.

In 2018, when I had to go into the St. Louis County municipal court system, I saw about 200 people in line waiting to have their time before the judge. The vast majority of people waiting to be seen were minorities. The question that came into my mind was if African Americans make up just a quarter of St. Louis County's population, why does it seem we are most of the "invited guests" in the courtroom?

There is a genocide—a lynching—that will catch us, whether we hang from a tree or hang in suspense as we wait for our children to come home alive.

As the pastor of the New Jerusalem Missionary Baptist Church in Ferguson, how do I preach love, forgiveness, and acceptance to a crowd who has been beaten, broken, humiliated, targeted for being different?

I just tell them that's exactly what Christ did for us.

2014

MARIE CHEWE-ELLIOT

I've been here before
Down through the ages
To this place, this stage
On the threshold of justice's door

Praying, marching, shouting
Knock, knock, knocking
Waiting and wading knee-deep then waist-high
through the tears of the mothers
knowing there will be others.
Praying, marching, shouting.
Yes, I have been here before
On the threshold of justice's door
Half a century ago
In Selma, Oxford,
And Birmingham.
Choking down indescribable rage
I gasp for air then
Dial 911 to resuscitate justice in New York, Sanford, Ferguson.
The call is unanswered and I know
The tears of the mothers will not bring them back
Marching, shouting, praying will not bring them back
There is no protection for driving while black, walking while black,
or just BE-ING black in America.
I can't breathe knowing there will
Be others.
Like Schwerner, Chaney, and Goodman
Emmett, Medgar, Martin,
Like Trayvon, Michael, and Eric
Who became casualties of war
On liberty and justice for some.
I have been here before
And the young ones say
We must dropkick the door.

Hands up and
hearts aflame
hold on to justice
Like nimbostratus
clouds hold rain.

Declaring never to visit
This place again.

What the Bullet Knows

VINCENT CASAREGOLA

Still new, the bullet knows,
innocently enough,
its own weight and heft,
solid and compact, smooth
and curved like a statue,
touched with power—
a totem or fetish.

The bullet learns,
soon enough, to be patient,
to wait in its tight jacket,
snug in its casing, waiting
with its brothers, all servants
to some deep and sudden will.

The bullet knows its own fire,
its sudden freedom of speed,
out in the open at last,
stinging the air till
that air itself is smoke,
wild with red and yellow light.

But the bullet is shocked
by its own trajectory and impact,
appalled at diving deep
into liquid red shadows,
into caves of bone that crack
like stalactites and shatter
downward into night.

The bullet cries out
in its own shattering demise
because it did not yet know

how to kill and die
in the same instant,
in a dozen jagged parts
fanning out, slowing down,
each tearing into its own red grave.

"You Have to Act Tough"

INDA SCHAENEN AND NORMANDY STUDENTS

When I moved to St. Louis in 1991, someone told me that to understand Missouri, you had to know that people here had strong opinions about three G's; God, guts, and guns—"guts" signifying reproductive freedom. God and guts aside, gun culture permeates our way of life. Depending on who you are, where you live, and what you do for a living, you might use guns for hunting, self-defense, family protection, intimidation, interpersonal problem solving, and exercising state power over unarmed citizens. You may not handle guns at all.

While I don't use guns, I do think about them. Since 2013, I've been teaching in the school district that graduated Mike Brown, who was shot on Canfield Drive, about three miles from our school, by police officer Darren Wilson. Last winter, my colleagues and I attended the funeral of one of our students, an eleventh grader, who had been shot by someone (we don't know who) on Christmas.

The deadly conflict between eighteen-year-old Mike Brown and twenty-nine-year-old Darren Wilson began with hostile words exchanged about where the unarmed teenager was walking. Wilson was driving an SUV, Brown was walking in the opposite direction. Wilson wanted Brown to move, to walk elsewhere, specifically on the sidewalk where a municipal code said that he, Brown, was supposed to be. Wilson yelled at Brown for violating an ordinance that mandates "a manner of walking." Ordinances like these fit into a centuries-long history of people who are white, with and without guns, attempting to regulate where people who are African American can walk, eat, attend school, shop, and work. Within two minutes, Mike Brown was shot dead and left in the street for four hours.

Four years later, in May 2018, students across the country were walking out of class to protest political leaders who would not pass laws restricting access to automatic assault rifles and other guns. My students and I were in North County. Almost every one of my students is African American. I'm white. It struck us that the gun control conversation didn't encompass the full history and texture of life with guns in St. Louis. We have active shooter drills in school. We discuss exactly what we plan on doing should the need arise. But

what about when we're not in school? My students hear gunshots as they fall
asleep at night. Some fear for their lives and the lives of their loved ones when
police officers are nearby.

And so, instead of walking out of school that day, these seventh and
eighth graders opened up laptops and wrote.

—*Inda Schaenen*

The reason that guns are out of control is because people fear being vulnerable. I feel like people need to understand that if one group of people stops making guns their first choice, then everyone will. It's like a game of monkey-see, monkey-do, and it's also not just in St. Louis. If our "leader" does one thing, then it will become okay for everyone to do it. This will always lead back to the government. If the cops have the right to walk around with big guns and feel like they have power, then people in the area around them will see that power and want some of it, too. People get tired of feeling powerless. So yes, they are going to jump to guns because you can never have a knife in a gunfight. This is the very reason why the gun laws that are going to be enforced on the community need to be enforced on the officers, too. And it's not just the fact that people can get guns like they get candy bars, it's the fact that people are not buying these guns to just have them. They are buying these guns because most of them have children to protect. When you're a kid, you are supposed to be able to go outside and run around freely without having to keep looking over your shoulder because you are scared of getting shot.

They carry guns to protect themselves from gangs in St. Louis. I also see guns while at stores and walking around with friends. I mainly see males with guns. Personal beef escalates to gun violence so quickly because people feel that others should be afraid of them. So they use a gun to threaten them, but when the other person has a gun they both want to show off. Once my sister got into an argument with some girls. Next thing you know, my sister and I are fighting a group of girls. A couple of days later they bust out my mother's car window and all of my sisters came over ready to fight. The whole street was outside waiting to see a fight. My brothers were out there with their guns and other men were outside with their guns. Before anyone started fighting, someone shot into the air and a shootout started to happen. My brother got shot in the leg and another girl got shot in her arm.

People don't get jobs to earn money, instead they kill for money. People can't provide for their family so they decide to kill for resources. People give this habitat/environment a bad look.

I have handled a gun. Somebody had just come from hitting a lick and when we were walking home, my brother and I, we went to see what was making noises. We found a gun. We took it home and examined it. After a week, my brother sold it and got rid of it. I feel like people just don't feel like being involved in a talking situation so they just end the bullshit right then and there.

People think that other people are going to shoot them, so they shoot them first. I feel bad for the people who get caught in shootings and the people who get shot for no reason. My grandma has a gun at her house because somebody broke into her house, so she got a gun.

I have seen plenty of guns. I think that people are turning to guns because they feel like people are not taking in what they are saying. I think conflicts escalate to guns so quickly because people feel like that's the only way that they are going to be respected. My stepdad got a gun because he was tired of telling the neighbor to back off and leave him alone. It's hard for people to live peacefully because no one is really willing to come out and say something about it and express the way that they feel about violence.

I was with my momma when I saw someone handle a gun. We had a block day for our family and someone was driving down the street very fast in an all-black car. My uncle is a very cautious person and he is our protector. So when he feels like his nieces and nephews are being harmed, he tries to harm someone. I think people turn to guns to solve their beef because it scares people. Some people see a gun and get scared so they leave the person alone. Some people try to act like they are not scared but really are and get shot. Living in St. Louis, Missouri, you have to act tough because if you don't, people will try to bully or harm you. I think personal beef escalates to gun violence so quickly because people are really hurt inside. Some people just take their anger out on anyone. That's why people shoot innocent people. I had an experience like that. My cousin's stepdad had so much anger built in him because of his mom's death. So one day he and a friend got in an argument at my aunt's house. My aunt was at work and me, my cousin, and his sisters and brothers were at my cousin's house. My cousin's stepdad went to grab his gun and he tried to shoot his friend, but the bullet bounced back and shot my cousin. Why is it so hard for people to live together peacefully? There is no answer to that question. No one will never know. People just have SO MUCH BAD STUFF BUILT IN THEM.

I have never handled a gun before and I don't plan to. It's just too much stress. I think people turn to guns because we've formed ourselves to think that guns are the only source of protection and that, "If he can use it, I can use it." "If he thinks it's cool, then it must be cool." Personal beef leads to gun violence because whatever they are upset about, they want to get rid of it so they turn to the only device they know and decide to get rid of it themselves. Peace is hard to gain because basically the stupid people in the world who just can't get it right are basically taking over the world. With our emotions and anger, we can't get along and understand how someone else is feeling, or we just don't care.

Gun violence escalates because some people are just crazy.

People are too weak to handle their problems by hand without using weapons, which shows that they're scared. People like to start drama over petty things like who ate my last cookie, then they be like, "Awe-ight, bet," then it's beef and it gets worse because they make posts instigating the fight, then eventually the violence starts with fistfights. Then the person gets beat up so they go for guns, knives, and other weapons and lay the other person in a hospital bed or six feet under the ground.

North St. Louis County
May 2018

All of the student contributors were, at the time of writing, seventh and eighth grade students in Normandy Schools Collaborative's Project Lab.

To A___ G___ in the Third Row

KATELYN DELVAUX

I hope your name never becomes a hashtag.
I hope your mother never has to defend your clothes,
or your time spent wandering the dark—
that teenage incubator where most of us learned to wait
and think and grow. I hope I never see your face
distorted, a picture from Halloween, four beers in
and feeling loose you cock your hands,
when for weeks you've sat at the back of my class,
thinking more than speaking, your papers a crescendo
waking. Your peers will blink at the cameras
and say you were always kind of quiet, but they will choose
someone you bumped in the hallway who knows you
were a thug. Your hat too blue,
your name too voweled. Piece by piece
they strip you for the audience, a vicious burlesque.
Remember the night you wanted to fit in,
the plague of ten-year-olds in new neighborhoods everywhere,
so you stuffed a soda in your jacket and ran like hell? They do.
One reporter finds your tweet about weed
and lifts it over her head, a trophy to hang.
Each piece plucked away until your bones lay naked,
still in the street where they left you, dull
in the pulse of candles and cop cars.
It is foolish to hope; you've known this
since your mother cried at the kitchen table
and explained that your legs must be concrete,
you must never run, that before you start
the car, you place your license on the dash—
never let them see you reach.
Your hand, a rocket slow to launch
behind a sea of vague haircuts and covert cellphones,
wants to know today's lesson,
and I hope you never learn it.

A Mother's Cry

DEBORA GRANDISON

Blood has been shed and so have the tears
creating expressions of mistrust, anger, hatred, and fear.

Many answers are needed to the questions
of why . . .
a mother is left crushed and heartbroken . . .
to grieve and to cry.

Violence and looting erupted . . . guns and gas masks applied
it cannot be forgotten . . . that a mother's son died.

It's now time to bring healing for the whole world to see
how great loss can bring change to this community.

Many offer their judgments not understanding the cause
that things aren't always equal for us
when it comes to the law.

Why does it seem no one's listening?
that they've turned a deaf ear
to the sobering cries of our mothers
year after year.

Many people desire to believe all is well
while those in the midst of the struggle view this as pure hell.

Is anyone willing to stand up for change?
or is it easier to see those living in turmoil as strange

Please don't be fooled my friends for there are still issues with race
the problem is: how do we close the gap and meet face to face?

You hear many speak out about their discontent
when viewing the actions of some who may misrepresent.

Remember we were created in love and love knows no bounds
whether black, white, red, or yellow . . . God's grace and mercy surrounds.

We must turn away from the falsehoods that the enemy breeds
and stand up in agreement to help those in need.

Caravan Waltz

ROBIN WHEELER

In 2014 it snowed the day before Thanksgiving in St. Louis. Big, fluffy flakes—the kind a local TV meteorologist once described as "hamster-sized" during a pre-blizzard panic several years ago. For years he used that description in his forecasts, even the night before, when his forecast was sandwiched into a newscast predicting whether our city would burn for a second night.

The snow didn't deter protestors who marched downtown, onto the highways in the shadow of Manifest Destiny's monument on the banks of the Mississippi, because a grand jury failed to charge the white police officer who shot and killed an unarmed black eighteen-year-old in August.

Bobbee Sweet killed it on 88.1 that afternoon with a soundtrack for driving through a broken city: an instrumental cover of "Mercy, Mercy Me," Marvin Gaye's original "Inner City Blues," and then Nomeansno's "All These Little Bourgeois Dreams," an introspection about driving all day to make a living, just to go home and watch television like a caged monkey.

The day before, a journalist in town for the verdict commented on how bourgeois I was because I worked in a gourmet shop. I sold Ozark black walnuts for a dollar an ounce, and bottles of the liquid-gold oil pressed from them packaged in bottles festooned with the international awards they'd won. The same filthy walnuts that used to litter my grandmother's yard, encased in green pods like tennis balls, but smooth, heavy, and hard. Deep inside, a rutted shell that didn't give up nuggets of meat without a hammer and a fight. I'd peeled back the green coats when I was a kid, stained my hands with the black resin inside, made a plaything out of the truffle of the Ozarks.

Bourgeois? Maybe. If making nine dollars an hour to sell nine-dollar bags of nuts made me an elite, fine. I knew I was privileged, one generation removed from a degree of deep Ozark poverty. The photos of my childhood home looked like they were taken in the 1800s, not sixty-five years ago. When people in the city were getting their first color televisions, my grandparents were finally bourgeois enough to afford indoor plumbing. My mother kept her childhood outhouse in her garden.

As I drove to work in the snow, Bobbee talked over a music bed of The Clash's "Guns of Brixton" before playing "Know Your Rights," the song that had looped in my head since August 14 when Michael Brown was murdered and the people started marching against police in military machines: "Murder is a crime. Unless it was done by a policeman."

Know your rights.

I'd listened to "Know Your Rights" that morning, trying to ease the residue of hearing "Brand New Cadillac" in a commercial for a car dealership that aired during last night's news. Maybe some kid, somewhere in St. Louis, caught the absurdity of selling Cadillacs to people under siege and realized that, in the spirit of the song, the bad guy's behind the wheel.

Because "The Weight" was used in a Diet Coke commercial when I was in my early twenties, I learned about The Band. The group backed Bob Dylan in the late 1960s and early 1970s while making their own music. Their songs "The Night They Drove Old Dixie Down" and "The Weight" earned them enough prestige to merit Martin Scorsese documenting their star-studded final concert in the film *The Last Waltz* on Thanksgiving, 1976.

Not that I knew this when it happened. I was four years old. I first heard "The Weight" in that commercial, which prompted me to buy their greatest hits CD and fall in love with a brand of music that sounded like home with its country overtones.

Every year on the night before Thanksgiving, Johnny Vegas and his brother Mark didn't let snow or fire stop them from hosting their tribute to *The Last Waltz*. Mark and Johnny were two of many, many siblings from an Irish-Catholic clan rooted in the inner ring west suburbs of the city. Raised on KSHE-95 Real Rock Radio and dogma, weed, and whippings, the two brothers shared a love of music. Mark got sucked into The Band through a VHS copy of *The Last Waltz* when he was a kid. Johnny got it a few years later when young MTV would play clips from the film as music videos. Their shared love of The Band continued into their adulthoods where their paths otherwise split—Mark's into a steady job, marriage, family, and Johnny's into booking bands, working in bars that always went out of business after hiring him, and conducting marriages in South City through the power vested in him by the Universal Life Church.

I knew Johnny from years of hanging out at bars and music venues in South City. He was a bartender whose bars always seemed to go out of business shortly after they'd hire him. Officially, we met one night when I staggered out of Off Broadway and screamed, "Hey! You're Johnny Vegas!" at him across the street. That's really all it took to become friends with Johnny.

Johnny met me at the door of 2720 Cherokee and wrapped me in a tight hug. I inhaled his aroma of several varieties of smoke and Stag beer, and he planted a kiss on my cheek. "You made it!"

That had become the *de rigueur* reaction when I managed to show up to anything. Months of depression from an unexpected heartbreak sent me into hiding in May. Live music further bruised my hurt heart, and the few shows I'd attended left me sobbing. And that was before my city shattered while we watched from the comfort of our living rooms, waiting to see how long Michael Brown's body would roast in the August sun on the asphalt, how big the war machines on South Florissant would be.

I burrowed deeper into my hole—how privileged to be lucky enough to choose to hunker down when, ten miles from my house, cops in armor stood with their weapons under the "Seasons Greetings" banner that stretched across the street by the Ferguson Police Department.

The grand jury's decision to not charge the cop who shot Mike yanked me out by the hair the night before *The Last Waltz*. Joining the protestors was out of the question. I couldn't afford to be in jail or injured, not with my ten-year-old child.

I moved through the still-quiet club, bought a beer from a bartender on the verge of her fourth trimester of pregnancy, and took a seat by myself near the big window. Cherokee Street, too, was desolate empty, despite it being one of the busiest bar nights of the year. With so much volatility that week, maybe people who came home for the holiday opted to nest with loved ones. Or maybe they allowed the news reports to frighten them.

I refused to be frightened of my city. The police were another story, but I had never been afraid of St. Louis. How could I be afraid of the place that housed the people who missed me when I was gone? The people who showed up for a gig despite the governor declaring a state of emergency? The people spanning seven decades in age who gathered to honor a moment in 1976 that left a mark on their souls? The bartender trying to earn tip money before the baby came? The club owner trying to keep the doors open?

The more it snowed and the later it got, the more people filtered in, many of them with the same broad noses, curly hair, and angular chins as Johnny and Mark. Their family was rumored to be related to William S. Burroughs, our local Patron Saint of Bad Decisions. Sister Miriam brought her new boyfriend, who was flinching and skittish at being among her large and boisterous family for the first time in their young relationship. "This is his practice run before meeting the whole clan tomorrow," she told me before saying it was good to see me out and about.

Levon Helm of the The Band grew up 300 miles south of St. Louis in Arkansas. He hunkered down back home in 1966 when the stress of being booed became too much. In his memoir he wrote that he'd gone back to the woodshed to decide what to do next.

We all need time in the woodshed. I did in 2014 for similar reasons, but on a smaller scale. Bob Dylan did it, too, at the same time as Levon.

It's good to be back, even if it took blatant, violent injustice to wake me up and remind me of the good in my city. Over forty musicians, willing to come out and play tribute to a relic despite the snow and the war in our city. Because it was good to see each other.

Three hours into the show, enough bodies filled the club to fog the windows. When "The King of France" threw open the door, a gust of frigid wind entered with him. He slid in on icy cowboy boots, having run the block from his bar just long enough to jump on stage and wail that the caravan has all my friends, turn it up, little bit higher, turn it up, that's enough so you know it's got soul, radio, radio turn it up, hum la la la la la la la . . .

We huddled in front of the stage, singing the words with him, as loud and enthralled as if he was a rock star and not just that guy from behind the bar at The Whiskey Ring, who was playing a little faster than usual because someone had to get back there to pour the drinks. But for five minutes, he was the King, saving us from the snow and fire, giving us reason to move—on the floor, off the couch, into the city where our caravan would stay parked, even if we needed to go to the woodshed or to march on Florissant Avenue.

Ferguson Protest Art Paid Forward

REBECCA RIVAS

Three days after Michael Brown Jr.'s death, De Andrea Nichols was leaving an Urban League Young Professionals event, suited in dress pants and a blazer.

The museum educator decided to head to the Ferguson Police Department to join the protests for the first time.

After a full night of chanting and drumming on the sidewalks, several armed vehicles and police dressed in riot gear formed a line before the group of about 200 civilians.

"I have never been confronted by a police officer," she said. "It was one of the most haunting moments."

In a video that Nichols recorded, one can hear activist Tef Poe shout out, "On your knees." They all fell to their knees and raised their hands, while several people prayed loudly for safety.

After that night, she had a reoccurring nightmare about black men carrying a closed casket covered with mirrors. It wasn't until she participated in several other actions that she came to the realization, "I have to build this."

In 2015, the Smithsonian in Washington D.C. purchase the mirrored casket, which made its debut during an action for Ferguson in October 2014. The Smithsonian's National Museum of African American History and Culture had been collecting artifacts and ephemera to document the Black Lives Matter movement.

In her view, Nichols said the piece challenges onlookers to reflect on their own roles in remediating the national crisis where countless young men of color die at hands of police and community violence.

"The object speaks a message that words don't fully articulate," said Nichols. "You could be in this casket. This could be your family. And then you look at yourself and you see that you are part of a system that is causing this."

After Nichols decided to build the casket, she emailed a group of artists about the idea. Those who responded became the casket team—Marcis Curtis, co-founder of the design studio Citizen Carpentry; Damon Davis, founder of the Far Fetched Collective and an interdisciplinary artist; Derek Laney, an organizer with Missourians Organizing for Reform and Empowerment;

Sophie Lipman, assistant registrar at the Pulitzer Foundation for the Arts; Mallory Nezam, director of STL Improv Anywhere; and Elizabeth Vega, the leader of the Artivists STL.

Curtis became the prime builder of the casket. From conception to finish, he said the casket took about ten days to come to fruition. Lipman and Nichols gathered supplies while Laney and Vega helped secure some funding for materials from Missourians Organizing for Reform and Empowerment.

Creating a casket of solid mirrors was beyond their budget, Curtis said, so he suggested a gunshot effect. To achieve that, he took a hammer to one of the big panels and then focused the mosaic mirror pieces around that point, he said.

The most time-consuming part—about eighteen hours—was the grouting, he said. The mirrors were attached with thick, white glue that left unappealing white seams. He wanted the mirrors to look like they were floating, so Curtis ran black latex caulk in every crack. Then he cleaned up each line with a straight razor.

With Nezam's art performance background, she said she was pushing for the casket to be presented in a candle-lit procession. The plan became to start at the Ponderosa Steakhouse parking lot (near Canfield Green), where Vega had built an altar, or *ofrenda*, based on the Mexican tradition of the Day of the Dead. The pallbearers, which included Laney and Davis, would carry the casket in silence to the Ferguson Police Department.

But that's not how it happened. The protests were roaring both near Canfield Green and at the police department, so silence was not in the cards.

"It took on a life of its own," Nezam said. "It had a lot more layers of meaning than we even realized."

Nezam felt the piece planted seeds of thought that night. Laney said he could feel the built-up grief and anger of the community reflected back through the mirrors. Nichols was admitted to the hospital that day, so she and Lipman proudly watched the casket's unfolding on social media in her hospital room.

Initially the group debated about whether they were ready to put the piece in a museum or to continue using it. They ultimately decided to sell it to the museum rather than giving it to the institution. Those negotiations have taken more than seven months, Nichols said, and the group has not yet disclosed the amount agreed upon.

"We decided we would not take any of the funding for ourselves but would find something comprehensive to continue using art as a catalyst for social change," she said. "Mass incarceration and how it affects the African American community is one of the most crucial civil rights pursuits of our time. It's using art in more transformative way."

Davis said he's glad the mirrored casket will be preserved, "so this moment isn't wiped away in history."

St. Louis Pride

RACHEL BRAND

Wait for the boys until you realize you don't care about the boys
Hear whispers about that part of the city
The part that is *you know, filled with those queer people*
You think those *queer people* are on to something
Girls who like girls? In my good Christian city?
You've no idea. There's so much light and so many drinks and so
Many people smoking cigarettes and now you get it
Now you understand what your place is and it's here with the drag queens
And the butch lesbians and the dykes and the twinks
And the older queer people who have lived through so much
This is home, finally, in this city where you lived and protested
The Westboro Baptist church and probably about
5-10 HELL IS REAL preachers.
Home is a strip of queer bars in a blue city in a red state.
With that cigarette in between your fingers and that drink in your other
hand
You realize that not caring about boys was *totally* worth it

My Brain Tumor

KIRSTEE PEMBERTON

Dedicated to the Doctors at Children's Hospital

Editor's note: St. Louis played a little-known role in the US government's push to develop nuclear weapons during World War II—the Manhattan Project. In the 1940s, raw uranium ore from the Belgian Congo went through initial purification at a facility in downtown St. Louis. A plot of land near the airport became a dumping ground for the radioactive waste left over from that process. Waste from that site contaminated Coldwater Creek, which flows through North County and frequently floods. A largely unknown amount of waste was later dumped at the West Lake Landfill in Bridgeton. Long-term exposure to low level radiation has been linked to cancer.

Kirstee Pemberton's family lives near the West Lake Landfill. In 2003, Kirstee was diagnosed with a rare form of brain cancer usually found in elderly men. A 2014 Missouri Department of Health and Senior Services study on cancer rates in the area found that Kirstee was one of seven cases of childhood brain cancer in her zip code. Statistically, there should have only been two.

Kirstee passed away in 2004. She was twelve. Her mother, Kirbi Pemberton, remembers:

> Kirstee was loving, caring, joyful, strong and one of the bravest little girls. We are so thankful to call her our daughter. She had a smile that could brighten a room and she taught many people the true value of life in her short journey. We are thankful for the twelve years of life that she had to enjoy the things she lived to do, such as, swimming, softball, gymnastics, hanging with her family and friends, and just being a kid. She left a memory that will last forever.

Kirstee wrote this story for a class assignment.

It was the beginning of the school year, and Kirstee was always having headaches. She would go down to the nurse, Mrs. Kretschmer's, office and get sent home.

Then one day, Kirstee's mom and dad picked her up from school, and had taken her to get an M.R.I.

When Kirstee and her parents got to the doctor's office they waited in the waiting room for Kirstee's turn. Finally, it was my turn. The nurse put Emla cream on my arm to make it numb. Kirstee asked, "What is the cream for?"

The nurse replied, "It's so you don't feel the shot."

Quickly I said, "What shot?"

"It's so we can get the right MRI results."

I agreed.

Kirstee was in the MRI machine for an hour. At least the doctor gave me headphones and put on my favorite radio station. The MRI machine made lots of loud bangs and booms.

After the MRI my parents and I again had to wait in the waiting room for the results of my MRI.

The doctors then called my mom and dad up and told them that I had a brain tumor and should go immediately to St. Louis Children's Hospital.

I asked my parents, "Why are we in such a hurry? What's wrong?" My mom turned around and said we had to go to the hospital because the doctors found something on my MRI and we have to let a doctor look at the films from my MRI.

When we arrived at the hospital, my parents had to fill out paperwork, and I had to see a neurosurgeon named Dr. Park and Dr. Alden.

They told my mom and dad that I would need to go into surgery tonight to relieve the pressure on my brain. So the nurse put me in a wheelchair so that I could be taken down for surgery.

Then my mom and dad told me I was going to have surgery. I began to cry, but my best friend Brooke's dad who works at St. Louis Children's Hospital and whose name is Louis told me, "Everything is going to be all right." He made me feel much better. Well it was time to go in for my surgery and my mom went in with me until I went to sleep.

When I woke up my mom and dad were in the room and my other family was in the waiting room. The doctors and nurses then moved me into a room in the PICU, which stands for Pediatric Intensive Care Unit.

The following day I went down for another scan to check the pressure on my brain before they could do my other surgeries. Everything looked good so they got me ready for my biopsy.

They took a biopsy of my tumor and it had both cells in it. It had malignant and benign cells. They even had to send it to the Mayo Clinic to have the results checked.

After being in the hospital for around two weeks, I was finally sent home and told that I would need to get radiation treatments.

After being home for a couple weeks, I began preparing for my radiation. I had to have a special mask made, so that when they would do my radiation they would know exactly where to shine the radiation to help shrink my tumor.

I had radiation five days a week for six weeks. My mom would pick me up from school early every day so that I could go and have radiation treatments at the hospital.

Since radiation, I have been going to the hospital every six months for an MRI. They want to see if the radiation is shrinking my tumor. It has shrunk a little! I have a tremor in my left hand, but I feel I'm doing well, and I'm a normal kid! I do well at school and sports, and love being me!

This is a Ramadan Story about How I Ended Up Crying in an IHOP

AISHA SULTAN

It's become a tradition in the St. Louis area for young Muslims to congregate at their nearest twenty-four-hour diner for a carb-olicious meal before the daily fast during Ramadan begins. In our area, this means showing up at the IHOP in Chesterfield Valley around 2:00 a.m. to finish eating around 3:45 a.m.

This is a relatively new tradition, started by the second and third generation Muslim teens growing up here. For some, the month-long fast from dawn to dusk may seem arduous, which it is, but it is also a time when fellowship among the Muslim community peaks.

Meeting at IHOP in the early hours of the morning seems like a lot of fun if you are young enough to stay up that late and still have the kind of metabolism to handle this sort of meal. I'm no longer among either demographic, but when my daughter wanted to go with her friends early one Saturday morning during Ramadan in 2018, I reluctantly agreed to drive them.

The restaurant was jam-packed with Muslims, mostly teenagers and college students, who seemed oblivious to the time. My eyes were burning, and I was debating whether I could really eat a 1,200-calorie breakfast. (It turns out, I could. Looking at you, spicy poblano omelette.)

I was lucky enough to join a friend who had arrived earlier and I got my food pretty quickly, but when I headed over to the girls' table, I realized their orders had not been taken and water had not been brought to the table despite nearly an hour wait.

It turns out Cedric, the manager on duty, was the only one serving this entire half of the restaurant. The other waiter had called in. Cedric was running around like a headless chicken. As the clock ticked closer to the end of suhoor time, I was getting more and more anxious about whether the kids would get any food before the fast started.

About fifteen minutes to the deadline, the tension was palpable with a roomful of hangry teens. Then the plates started rolling off the order counter—strawberry and cream, Cinn-a-Stack pancakes and hash browns that got doused in hot sauce. Thankfully, everyone got their food and was able to scarf it down in time.

When we were getting up to leave, I realized what an intense situation it is for the waitstaff during these early morning hours of Ramadan, especially if a coworker doesn't make it in. I wondered if the young people knew how important it was to tip the waitstaff well and that certain circumstances are beyond the control of the servers. I called Cedric when I got home and thanked him and said I would come by later with an additional tip.

He said the phone call meant more to him than an extra tip.

I shared my thoughts about what the waitstaff deals with during this month on a few local Muslim social media groups. It kicked off a spirited discussion about raising awareness within our community about tipping. Immediately, people said they wanted to contribute toward a small bonus to show our appreciation. Within twelve hours, people had sent me money via Venmo and Paypal, and when I showed up for an iftar at the mosque that evening, women literally shoved cash at me to take to the servers.

After we broke our fast, I drove by the IHOP around 10:00 p.m. I asked if I could speak to Cedric. He didn't remember who I was until I reminded him that I had called and was worried about whether he and the staff were tipped appropriately.

Then I handed him two envelopes with nearly $1,000 inside and said, "This is from the St. Louis Muslim community to thank you and the waitstaff for feeding us during those 2:00 a.m. shifts during Ramadan."

Cedric was stunned. His jaw dropped. His eyes got red and watery. And he said, "Just the phone call was enough. Really, that was enough."

At a time where it seems like communities are increasingly fractured and divisions are inflamed, moments like these remind me of the things that connect us.

Ramadan is about more than physically abstaining from food and drink. It's about nurturing our connection to a force greater than us and to one another. The predawn and evening meals are about more than refueling your body, they are about feeding your soul. That morning, Cedric's plight moved me and inspired an entire community.

And that my friends, is how I ended up in tears in the International House of Pancakes.

(PSA: Always tip your waitstaff well.)

"This is a Ramadan Story about How I Ended Up Crying in an IHOP" was first published in the St. Louis Post-Dispatch.

The Syrians Come to Hodiamont

ROBERT LANGELLIER

At the dinner to benefit Syrian refugees, there aren't enough seats for the Syrians. The room at the Boo Cat Club is packed, and Jessica Bueler is flitting around, managing the event, making sure that the crowd of equally white St. Louis women is enjoying the food. A young Syrian boy stops her and quietly asks where he's allowed to sit.

"Anywhere," Bueler says, smiling, continuing on.

The boy walks back to where his family of five is standing pinned against the side wall of the event and whispers something to his dad. His dad looks as if he were told to sit in every seat at the same time. Bueler catches this and zips over, leading the family to a central table where she asks spread-out diners to scooch together.

This is Bueler's thirteenth Supper Club dinner, in which she invites St. Louisans to pay twenty-five dollars for the chance to eat home-cooked Syrian food and meet a few of the sixty-eight Syrian refugee families that have been resettled in St. Louis since 2014. Six of them cooked this evening, and all the night's proceeds will go to them.

In 2016, Bueler founded the grassroots organization Welcome Neighbor STL after she was horrified by a *Riverfront Times* story detailing the beating of teenage Syrians in North City, and she's been rallying St. Louisans to provide support for refugees ever since. Playing the role of pep-rally leader, she uses loud and ESL-friendly language to introduce the audience to the evening's cooks, who announce what they've cooked—shawarma, kibbeh, fattoush, tabouleh, hummus—and stand awkwardly for the accolades. The thrum of applause thermals into a frenzy when Alifa Alahmad, a young woman in a floral hijab, steps forward and says the word "baklava."

Three of the Syrian cooks live in the Garden Apartments near Hodiamont and Page, about a mile north of Delmar. The block, which adjoins Amherst Park, features the splintered and rotted bones of old homes and a too-wide street paved with more traffic in mind. I used to (unwisely) describe areas of East St. Louis as "like Syria." This neighborhood was no better. This is the neighborhood where some Syrian teens were beaten in 2016, drawing Bueler's attention. A dozen or so refugee families have left the area already. The ones who remain haven't had the choice.

The day before the welcome dinner, no fewer than eleven Syrians greet me in a living room with tea, kibbeh with olive oil and za'atar, olives, makdous, labneh, and Arabic coffee set on a tablecloth on the floor.

Apparently still shocked by the violence they've witnessed in North City, the group ticks off a list of what they've experienced collectively at the Garden Apartments in the last two years: the beating of their teenagers, a holdup at gunpoint, two cars smashed in by baseball bats, a chilling attempted kidnapping of one of their daughters, a rock thrown through their living room window, kids hit with baseball bats, a stolen bicycle, a man creeping around with a stocking mask on (two weeks ago), men breaking into their living room wielding a Taser (one week ago). The wives stay awake until their husbands get home, sometimes as late as 2:00 a.m. They've called 911 so many times that dispatch provided them with a special number to call.

Then there are the living conditions themselves. A roach crawls across the floor. Iman Alkrad, one of the Supper Club cooks, casually picks it up with a paper towel and kills it. Soon after, I spot another across the room, on the wall. Later, they show me a five inch by ten inch sticky trap plastered with fully 1,000 insects. They inform me that this trap is today's. As in *only* today's. Happily, winter put a break on the bed bug infestation that had attacked their children's legs. "When I leave, I'll only take our clothes and some kitchen tools," says Iman Alkrad, the matriarch of the small Syrian community.

"Everything else is going to waste," her husband Ammar says. "The roaches are inside the furniture."

With an invisible grace, Alahmad and Najlaa Alsaadi take my dishes, sweep away the dinner crumbs, and clean the apartment before I even notice.

Some have suggested that the Syrians' problem in North City is cultural. In 2016, Jeffrey Boyd, the alderman for this ward, suggested to KMOX that perhaps if the Syrians didn't eat their meals on the floor, they might not have an insect infestation. The same week, KSDK's Jason Aubry wrote, "A number of those (cockroach and field mice) problems can be associated with the refugee [sic] themselves not knowing or understanding how things work here in the Midwest, surrounded by an abundance of bugs and animals foreign to them."

One might suggest the problem here is capitalist. Our system incentivizes landlords to take advantage of renters with, say, no English proficiency, few to no community ties and nowhere else to go—and therefore no ability to complain. The families blame the insect infestation on their landlord neglecting to cut the grass, and they claim he one day tried to resolve a mold issue by painting over it. (Their landlord says this is not true.) As for the alderman, Boyd, Jessica Bueler maintains that he has offered no more than lip service about helping the Syrians. Boyd did not respond to an interview request.

"Conflict is normal between people," Abu Osama, who lives at the Garden Apartments, says. Osama is thin with penetrating eyes. "We've been through trouble back home, but people figure things out. Here, it's so easy for people to pull out a gun. I've seen so many people pull guns out flippantly. I've seen someone shoot someone in the leg just down the street. I've seen someone get shot at a gas station just a couple weeks ago."

"We left death and came to another death," the Alkrads' son Mohammad says.

"We're not asking to live in Clayton," Ammar Alkrad interposes, already keenly aware of the places a St. Louisan might aspire to. "Just a better place, something better than this." Despite their frustrated comments, the Alkrads clarify that they're grateful to be in St. Louis, where they have found the people far more welcoming than those they experienced in Jordan. Here they have the chance to make a life, even if it's one starting from Hodiamont.

The Dar Al-Jalal mosque and Welcome Neighbor STL have worked to relocate Syrians from Garden Apartments to other parts of the city and county. The mosque paid to help with families' leases for one year, while Welcome Neighbor STL raised $15,000, providing $1,000 to each moving family to help subsidize the new residences. Only three remain. The money is there, Bueler says; the complication is a matter of rehoming large families with several children. After getting the Syrians out, Bueler says she wants to focus on Somali families living at the Garden Apartments, who are also facing violence.

Until mounting back rent forced her to shutter in March, Bueler owned HSB Tobacconist on the Loop; her father founded the business in 1972. Although she founded Welcome Neighbor STL long before closing HSB, the vacuum that followed the tobacco store's closure has shifted Welcome Neighbor STL into overdrive, for the Syrians at Hodiamont and beyond. Bueler recently designed curricula for twice-weekly English lessons for eighteen Syrians at Grace United Methodist Church, organizing pickup, dropoff and daycare services for mothers. The Supper Club she founded has also exploded; Welcome Neighbor STL has received so many recent requests that they've had to put a temporary hold on reserving the cooks.

Bueler stepping in with Welcome Neighbor STL has been a lifeline for the families still at Hodiamont. But the situation continues to rankle. What has been discouraging, Ammar says, is that their section of the apartment complex was where all the incidents occurred, and yet they have been the ones who've proven too difficult to rehome quickly. "We've become part of the past tense now," he says. "People and the media have forgotten about us."

Abu Osama, who has five children, fixes on me intently. He has heart problems stemming from the war in Syria. Certificates earned by some of the young children in school hang on the wall, opposite a boarded-up window. Two of the men in the room in their early twenties hadn't been to a single day of class since the Arab Spring began, and are now working full time to support their families.

"We don't want food or water," Osama says. "We just want our kids to be safe and have a good life. That's all we want. Our future is gone. Now we need to take care of them."

The guests are savoring their baklava. Bueler, standing at the head of the room, calls attention and gives thanks to everyone involved, to applause. She announces the next Supper Club event. Then she indicates the woman standing next to her, Iman Alkrad.

"Iman would like to share a story with you all. Iman, do you want to talk about your first day in St. Louis?"

Alkrad speaks haltingly to accommodate a translator. "It was a bad day," she says. "I was crying. I traveled a long distance. It's been seven years since I've seen my daughters. I felt scared. And after I met people here and Jessica came to visit me at home with the group, with Susan, they became like my family, like sisters. They helped us, thank God."

In the pauses during translations, Alkrad returns to Daraa, on the southern tip of Syria. She fled in February 2013 with blankets and kitchen tools, her home demolished, leaving one daughter behind. It was two years after the outbreak of Syrian unrest, 700 days of bloodshed. One day, during Eid al-Adha, one of Islam's most important holidays, an explosion shook the city. A car bomb had gone off outside a restaurant where children were playing. Blood and flesh flew everywhere. Children and women screamed. Iman's kids had only just left the area to come home.

Another time, Alkrad's twenty-one-year-old nephew's house was shelled. His one-month-old daughter survived with a broken leg. They found the mother in pieces in the bathroom. The father's head exploded on the living room carpet.

Alkrad fled with her family to the Jordanian desert, where they lived for two months in a tent camp. The tents were candlelit and would sometimes catch fire, burning up their inhabitants. Because there was no security in the camp, rape was common; someone always kept watch through the night.

It was there they learned that Iman's mother-in-law, trapped in a basement in Syria, had suffocated from the fumes of a gas bomb. Eventually Alkrad's family smuggled themselves out on a bus and got onto a list for UN refugee resettlement, from which Alkrad and her husband were sent to St. Louis.

"I wish I could hold my daughter," Alkrad says. "I don't know if I'll see her again. I don't know if I'll see my brothers. Only God knows. Inshallah [God willing]."

Alifa Alahmad, who is standing next to Alkrad at the dinner and preparing to speak, suddenly finds herself back in Aleppo, site of the brutal four-year Battle of Aleppo between the Syrian military and opposition forces. No one left their shelled homes; snipers hiding in the ruins fixed on anything that moved. A pregnant woman in labor finally ventured outside, holding a white rag as a sign of peace, desperately looking for a place to give birth. They shot her.

Alderman Boyd, in a separate 2016 interview with KMOV, argues that violence terrorizes his whole ward, not just the Syrians living in it. It's a fair point. Many have lived their entire lives amid violence. The question becomes a nebulous one, one of quantifying St. Louis's complicated violence: Do the Syrians, who did not grow up in this community, deserve to leapfrog black residents, who have suffered centuries of racial and economic discrimination, into a safe neighborhood?

And yet in Syria, at least these families were thrust into a chaos for which they had context. Here in north St. Louis they are not only scared, but culturally lost. For those born here, the world expands at the rate at which we speak to others, unfolding their worlds into our own. For a refugee who doesn't know the language, the world is fixed to the size of how many other Syrian refugees are around them. At Hodiamont, the world has shrunk to the size of three families.

It's not the poverty or the bed bugs' bite that overwhelms. It's the unfulfilled promise of peace, the anxiety of red memories that never leave, and the new alien fear that every brushed hair, itch, tic, or any other minute sensation is a bed bug or roach that eventually overwhelms.

Najlaa Alsaadi, another of the Supper Club cooks, speaking of Syria, later tells me: "It never escapes us, never escapes our mind. I was just on the phone with my mother yesterday. She said she wishes she can hold me, and I started crying, and she started crying. Even after we hung up, she called me again five minutes later, just to tell me to stop crying."

The Supper Club event is winding down. Those Americans who came with friends are leaving; those who managed to introduce themselves to Syrians are still chatting excitedly with them. At the end of one table, next to the plundered remnants of food trays, Maysaa Telmesani speaks into a cell phone, waiting for Google Translate to perform its charms. She then passes it to the woman across from her, who looks at the English and laughs.

"This is the thing that's empowering them to take the next step, to talk to people, to give them the confidence to use English, and to actually make money," Bueler says. Supper Club serves all of these ends.

Telmesani, a Syrian teacher, arrived in the US four hours before Trump's Muslim ban took effect. A week later, Telmesani receives the chance to teach again for one hour at Mallinckrodt Academy, a South City school for the gifted. In front of a crowd of bored, relatively affluent young children, Telmesani shows the children a slideshow photo of her once-upon-a-time Syrian students. Then she wrings from her nascent English vocabulary the story of Daraa, where the Syrian revolution began on March 6, 2011.

"Some students—I think that they were at the same age as you— in Daraa," she says, "wrote some words in the street. The statement . . . the meaning of the statement in English was, 'Dr. Bashar, your return is coming.'

"An officer in Daraa—he was the cousin of the president—he took these students who wrote these statements and took them to a place. We can say it was a prison. They force fear on them and kill them and take their [finger]nails from their places. He took their nails."

Schoolchildren seldom give public speakers serious attention, especially if the speaker is an adult with a thick accent. Yet several of the students here gasp, locked onto Telmesani. One young girl gapes for the rest of the hour, horrified. Telmesani goes on to describe how Syrian officials broke her father's skull. One of the teachers raises her eyebrows and glances at the students, concerned yet ultimately unwilling to stop this grown woman tearing up in front of children she's met this week.

There's a fantasy that refugees, once they arrive, start life anew. But of course they don't. They continue living, and every time gunshots ring out in North City, a family member, a friend, or a pregnant woman holding a white flag dies again, and the past keeps knocking on the door of the future.

Since the Supper Club event at the Boo Cat Club, Alifa Alahmad and her family have relocated from the Garden Apartments to a home in Crestwood. Three families remain, including Iman and Ammar Alkrad's, waiting for the war to end.

Quotations from Arabic were translated by Sara Bannoura. "The Syrians Come to Hodiamont" was first published in the Riverfront Times.

I wonder how many

MAJA SADIKOVIC

(of my)
people feel
just ok.

St. Louis Co. Cuts Mental Health Funds

MATTHEW FREEMAN

I stood in line on Lindell
waiting for a burger
safe from the wind and rain
ready to take my PRN

having cashed my check earlier
when I saw a guy out
the window waving his arms
and coming towards the door.

The line was long and I stayed put.
The man came in wet and disheveled
mumbling about the government
and went over to the condiment stand.

Among the whispers and managers
and the regulations and fever looks
he mixed packets of ketchup into water
to make some kind of hobo soup.

I wasn't grand, I nearly cared, I left
with my burger practically free.
But as I crossed the threshold glancing back
I thought: soon that could be me.

"St. Louis Co. Cuts Mental Health Funds" was first published in Dogtown Poet.

Carpenter, Branch

JOSH BURBRIDGE

Oh no. Almost 9:00. Going to be late.

Five blocks to go. If I don't run, Julia will give me that look. God, the heat bouncing off the pavement is unbearable.

I walk through the unlocked back doors, sweating, at 8:57. The gentle roar of the AC does more to comfort me than the air, which is far from cool. We have no control over the thermostat. Central Library downtown manages that. We're just a branch. But as most St. Louisans understand, even though the beloved Busch Stadium is there, downtown is not really the heart of St. Louis. It's in neighborhoods like this one throughout the city and region. Branch libraries may as well be their town squares.

"Good morning," I say to no one in particular.

"Josh! Don't forget to turn on the reference monitors."

"Thanks, Scott. We'll take care of them." Scott is a custodian. For some reason he speaks to me like he's my supervisor. I think he wants my job more than I do. Meanwhile, he runs a semi-wet cloth slowly across the counter, leaving a streak. The counter looks less clean than before.

Darrell, the other custodian, comes up behind him and shakes his head. "How you doing, Josh?"

"I guess I'm doing all right."

"Good to hear. That's a blessing."

I log on to my computer behind the counter, preparing for the storm. Trying to find at least one second to breathe, find peace, and get ready mentally. This is going to be a long day.

"Josh, did you turn on the reference monitors?"

"No, not yet. Sorry, Julia."

"I got them already," Keith chimes in, rolling his eyes at the question. Like many at the library, he is overqualified and underappreciated.

"Jesus, they're lining up already. Here we go."

"It's 9:00. It's 9:00! Unlock the door," commands Julia.

At the Carpenter Branch of the St. Louis Public Library, located at the south end of the South Grand business district, the onslaught, at nine dollars an hour, begins.

Within seconds the front lobby is filled with a long line of patrons.

Some already seem agitated. And the questions—the same ones over and over—begin.

"Well, to get on a computer you need a library card," I reply to a patron.

"What do I need to do to get a library card?"

"It's easy. Just need a current ID and proof of address." Getting regular compliance on this request is often harder than it sounds.

"Oh, okay. Here you go."

"Thank you. Is this your current address?"

"No, I moved." Many of our patrons move around a lot, leading to consistent card problems.

"Well, if your current address isn't on your ID, we'll need some proof of current address—a bill, for instance."

We just need to see something—almost anything, really—that makes a logical connection. Once, a woman desperate to get a library card for her child (another situation where corroborative documentation is needed) tried to use a tattoo of the child's name and birthdate as proof. We had to call downtown for that one. Reluctantly, we asked her to come back with something more "official," but we were impressed with her ingenuity.

"Oh. Well, that's it. I still live there. That's my address."

I know I've just been lied to, and it hurts a little, but this time I am just going to roll with it. Turns out he already has an old card account, anyway. "Well, to unlock your card you'll either need to return a missing item or pay the fine."

"What missing book? I don't have any missing books."

"Actually, let me turn my monitor around to show you." "That? I returned that!"

"I'm sorry, sir, but this dates to 2006. It would have turned up."

"Okay, fine. How much?"

"Forty-three dollars."

"Forty-three dollars! Oh my god, you're killing me. I just need to get on a computer."

"I'm sorry."

Over and over again, they come. Elderly. Young. Some too young to be coming to the library by themselves. Some so old that you marvel how they managed to take the bus to get here. White, black, rich, poor, middle class, and very poor. Owners of historic mansions with good jobs, and roaming homeless just looking for a break from the heat. Thousands of questions, left and right.

"Envelope."

"Sorry?" I reply, confused.

"I need an envelope," the young woman says, annoyed, straightening the papers in her hands in preparation.

"Do you have an envelope?" She enunciates each word.

"No, sorry."

"You don't have *any* envelopes back there."

We have might have some envelopes, but sadly I had to learn that at the library, once you start to give things away, people expect them every time. I gave in once to a young man who each day asks for hand sanitizer. After that, the branch manager told me to tell him to go wash his hands in the bathroom. I wonder if he's the one who turned over the trash can in there the other night. He still asks.

"Sorry. No envelopes."

"White out?"

"No, ma'am, we're a library. People will mess up the books."

"Okay, well I just need to fax this."

"We actually don't have a fax machine."

"*You don't have a fax machine?* Where am I supposed to fax this?"

"I'm sorry, but we don't have one. FedEx at Grand and Arsenal does."

"But I'll have to pay for it!"

Sigh. "Yes. I'm sorry."

Next, a woman in her twenties walks up. She smiles at her baby pleasantly as she pushes a giant stroller full of thin, oddly-shaped children's books. We scan and mark each one as returned, then we sort and route them to different branch libraries throughout the city. In doing so, I sincerely believe that I have faithfully served the citizenry of St. Louis, if only in this very small way.

Thirty minutes later the same woman walks up with her baby and the same stroller, which is now overfilled with several brand new stacks of children's books that she proceeds to plop on the counter.

"I see here you have one book out and overdue. *Good Night Gorilla*," I say, looking at her account. "Do you want to pay the fine on that?"

The mood changes drastically.

"*What?* I *just* returned that."

"In the books you brought in a few minutes ago?"

"Yes. I'm *certain* it was in there. I *definitely* returned it."

Did we miss it? She's standing straighter, looking at me directly as if to say, "I do not have time for this shit." Her respect for me is evaporating.

I am thankful for the counter between us.

"Ma'am, we scanned in all of those books. Are you sure you returned it?"

"Yes, I am."

My coworkers and I frantically look for the book. Maybe Audrey or Kyle quietly shelved it already. Meanwhile, the woman is getting more and more perturbed, as are the other waiting patrons, who seem to multiply exponentially. Alan and Peter come from the back to help, while Colleen eyes the situation with concern. Julia watches the whole situation closely with her arms crossed. I feel trapped.

Honestly, we very well may have missed it, and the woman just as likely did not "definitely" return it. No one really knows, at least right away. She's mad, we're stressed, and there's a loss of trust all around. All over *Good Night Gorilla.*

"Okay, well, the assistant manager asked if you could check at home again and we'll see if it turns up here."

"Fine." She walks away annoyed. She'll be back, and who knows what will happen.

Thank god, it's lunchtime. Maybe I'll walk up to the coffee shop. No, I shouldn't spend the money; I'll just a walk around the neighborhood. The hour flies by, and too soon I am right back behind the counter.

"Oh, hello. Can I help you?"

A group of about two dozen slightly nervous people walks in. Their arrival at Carpenter, it turns out, is a product of the International Institute, a century-old organization that works to ease the resettlement of immigrants in St. Louis. In the span of an hour we hear numerous languages—Portuguese, Arabic, Chinese, Spanish, and more—as we do our best to help. One man from Somalia has mastered enough English to flirt with Nirmala, while another man with piercing eyes from Afghanistan is one of the few possessing the required identification to get a library card. I can only wonder what story his story is.

South St. Louis, home to the Carpenter Branch, has changed substantially in recent decades, and the library's collection has evolved with it. An influx of refugees from Bosnia-Herzegovina that settled in the nearby Bevo Mill neighborhood in the 1990s prompted the creation and expansion of a Bosnian-language section to serve that community. But in just one generation, much of the Bosnian population left the city for suburban south St. Louis County, leaving behind a smaller, aging community, a few restaurants, and several shelves of largely unused books.

"Hi!" says a smiling man in glasses as he walks through the door.

"Oh, Mr. Lee is here. His papers are behind the reference desk," Mark says. As a member of the burgeoning community that helped define the South Grand and Gravois area in the 1980s and 1990s, Mr. Lee, a thin, graying man in his sixties, represents another part of the area's recent evolution. The staff happily saves copies of one imported newspaper for Mr. Lee, who gratefully picks up stacks of them after saying hello to the entire staff. But as the local Vietnamese community ages and dwindles in numbers, fewer and fewer Vietnamese patrons access the branch's substantial collection of Vietnamese literature. Thus, it is very possible the library unintentionally purchases the very expensive paper solely for Mr. Lee.

Perhaps the most significant demographic change on the south side has been the movement of thousands of African Americans to the area. Previously shut out of that part of town by residential segregation, many have fled the crime and poverty of parts of the north side in search of safety and stability. Accordingly, the curators of Carpenter's collection strive to serve them better. One genre, urban fiction, has grown so popular that it has warranted the creation of its own section in a prominent, highly visible position. It's a fascinating evolution that makes one believe in librarians as community servants.

Luckily, I get to sit next to Connie at the reference desk for a few minutes. A brilliant woman in her fifties and a native of the city's Central West End, Connie provides the branch's sharpest—and most hilarious—observations about local politics, film, history, and neighborhood personalities. Her scratchy voice is like none other, blessing you with nothing but straight, refreshing honesty—always followed by a childlike giggle.

"I saw your friend over there earlier," she says smiling, referring to one regular patron, a long-haired man wearing blue medical scrubs though he does not work in the medical profession.

"Yeah, he's usually really nice and talkative, but today he was acting strange. Like he was mad at me or something."

"Uh-huh. They'll turn on you. He's been coming in here for years. Some of these people are nuts. They don't have anywhere else to go."

Just then I notice a man in the computer lab accessing semi-nude photographs.

"Excuse me, sir. Sir. *Sir!*" I say, struggling to get his attention. He takes off his headphones and looks at me blankly. "You can't look at that here."

"I wasn't doing anything."

"Sir, I *saw* what you were doing. It's against library policy. Please stop it now."

Just then, I hear Steve exclaim from the front desk, in a whisper, "Josh! Come here! I've got something to show you."

An extremely popular constant at Carpenter for two decades, Steve is arguably the branch's most unforgettable figure. Many patrons ask for him by name, while others fondly ask for "you know, the guy with the hair," referring to Steve's unmistakable, though uniquely fashionable, spiky gray and white mop. He's also the main supplier of the candy drawer in the back room.

A St. Louis lifer, Steve has spent most of his life just a few blocks north of the branch near Tower Grove Park, an increasingly fashionable area where homes can go for over $400,000. That's not the world he inhabits, though; he's part of a distinctive yet fading vernacular version of the city. He spent his early childhood on the north side, a part of town that's his true and absolute love.

"I have a house for you."

"Okay, let me see it," I say smiling, knowing this is going to be interesting.

He shows me a picture online. It's gorgeous. Of course, it needs so much more work and money than I could ever give it. "Where is it?"

"Well, it's on Strodtman . . . near the water towers," an area that for decades has struggled with crime and dereliction.

I shake my head, still smiling. "I'd love to, but . . ."

"It's only $5,000, and it needs a good owner. Look! Beautiful!"

"But, Steve, there's a giant hole in the roof."

"Well . . . ," he trails off, shrugging as he holds his vintage horn-rimmed glasses with both hands. He smiles lightly because he knows. He still tries, though. He still fights for his city.

Steve's hopefulness puts me in a good mood, as does the fact that it's nearing 6:00. Almost time to go.

"Josh, Patrick just called in. Can you stay until 9:00 tonight?"

I've made it this long, so I guess I can survive until close.

Jessica and I pass the time with whispers about the management and our dreams—less stressful jobs. She's thinking about making the jump to be a dental hygienist or maybe even giving in and becoming a career librarian. Most of all, she dreams of being a writer, but long days at the library mixed with a second job at Target leave little room for creative expression. Several years older than her, I still have no idea what I'm going to do. Maybe this is where I belong.

It's dark outside now, and numerous fluorescent lights both illuminate the building and rob it of warmth and color. Thankfully, we get to hear Berra, a sheriff's deputy, and Hall, a city park ranger, joke around in between views of their phones. Some truly crazy people walk through those doors, so it's comforting to know guys like Berra and Hall are there to keep us as safe. They also keep rowdy kids in line. As a group of three run by the front desk, Berra unexpectedly breaks his smile and our conversation to let out a booming "Walk!" that shakes them to the core. They listen and they walk.

It's 8:45, and in fifteen minutes we'll all be set free. Joan, a retired veteran of the library who dedicated her career to teaching children, arrives to give Connie a ride home. They often stop at Ted Drewes in Dutchtown on the way to their respective far south side homes. Joan's bright smile tells me the end is near. She and Steve exchange playful barbs as only old friends can. It's a beautiful thing to witness.

The computers begin logging off automatically. Numerous people file out of the lab and we breathe a sigh of relief. One woman, though she has had multiple warnings that the lab would be closing soon, is ticked. "I was in the middle of something."

"Did you save it?"

"No! Isn't there *some way* I can get it back?"

"No, ma'am, we're sorry."

"There's *no way*?"

"No, ma'am."

"There's *nothing* you can do?"

She sighs loudly and fumes as she turns for the doors. I'm a little worried she's going to call downtown and complain. People do that all the time. Even though I'm right, a phone call to Central won't look good on my record.

"I'm sorry," I say to her. "You'll have to come back tomorrow and start over."

St. Louis, a Portrait from 2010

NARTANA PREMACHANDRA

I had just made a colossal error.

"We do not celebrate the *Chinese* New Year," the Taiwanese organizer told me politely. "We are from *Taiwan*. We celebrate the *Lunar* New Year."

I blushed under my rouged cheeks, curved my deeply red lips into a smile.

"I'm so sorry," I said, in a very apologetic tone, "It's just that last week I danced at the Chinese Buddhist temple for the Chinese New Year. I meant to say, thank you for inviting us to perform at your *Lunar* New Year celebration."

The gentleman nodded. But didn't say anything. I knew what he must be thinking: *You Americans are all the same!*

It was 2010. We—Dances of India, my mom's classical Indian dance company—had been invited to perform at the Taiwanese Cultural Center in a church in Chesterfield, a nicely manicured and increasingly diverse epitome of suburbia. The performance was for their Lunar New Year celebration, which I had just mistakenly called "Chinese New Year."

I indeed had just performed the week before in a refurbished church in Maryland Heights, which was now the Fo Guang Shan St. Louis Buddhist Center. For the first time in my life, I performed a classical Indian dance piece—portraying Avalokiteśvara, the Tibetan Buddhist deity of compassion—for an audience that was mostly Chinese.

Talk about multiculturalism. The Buddha now peacefully sat where the Virgin Mary, or perhaps Christ himself, once gazed meditatively at the bowed heads of the faithful. I had thoroughly enjoyed the experience, complete with vegetarian Chinese takeaway meals.

But I was a little concerned about this show—how would it go, in a Taiwanese church, when I'd started off by making such a politically incorrect mistake?

It turned out I had no need to worry.

The Taiwanese—most of whom spoke little English—whooped it up for the South Indian folk dance I performed. It's true, the rhythms were intoxicating, but I like to think the story of the piece was what really set the audience on fire. Sung in Kannada, the language of the Indian state of Karnataka, the dance described a pot.

I did everything possible with the pot—placed it on my head and stamped rhythmically on the floor, turned it over in my left hand, and drummed upon the hollow bottom with my right, and carried it in both my hands as I swayed and spun upon the floor.

This pot was a miraculous pot. If you cleaned it—or even if you didn't—it shone. It didn't matter if it was brass, silver, or copper. It still shone. So what's the story behind this pot?

The pot represents the human soul. The piece is an old folk tune sung in the villages, and was supposed to have been written ages ago by a Muslim living in a mostly-Hindu environment. As with so many songs and works of art in India, the author is unknown.

The audience at the Taiwanese church loved it. Afterwards, one of the attendees even asked the meaning of the refrain, which she then mouthed in pulverized Kannada.

The moment struck me. A Taiwanese Christian speaking a Kannada sentence written by a Muslim villager to a Hindu from St. Louis?

Flyover country's become, well, kinda fly.

ACKNOWLEDGMENTS

The St. Louis Anthology was made possible with the support of:

Imo's Pizza

STL-Style

Missouri Humanities Council

This book could not have happened without Anne Trubek's enthusiasm, Dan Crissman's guidance, and the dedication of the entire team at Belt. Additionally, I'd like to thank the friends and family whose ideas, perspectives, and thoughts helped shape this book, and whose encouragement and love kept me moving: Kevin Whiteneir Jr., Tori Lee, Ray Long, Jo Herrera, Cameron Powell, Abbey Blue, and others.

Most importantly, I'd like to thank the contributors. This anthology belongs to them.

—Ryan Schuessler

CONTRIBUTORS

Alonzo Adams, born in St. Louis and raised in Ferguson, is a graduate of the University of Missouri and a veteran of the United States Navy. He is the pastor at New Jerusalem Missionary Baptist Church in Ferguson and lives in Florissant with his wife Ronica and their four children.

Chris Andoe is editor in chief of *Out in St. Louis* and a longtime columnist for *Vital Voice*. He is the author of *Delusions of Grandeur*.

Samuel Autman began his newspaper career as a carrier for the *St. Louis Post-Dispatch* when he was in the fifth grade. He began writing for newspapers at the *Tulsa World,* the *Salt Lake Tribune*, the *St. Louis Post-Dispatch* and finally the *San Diego Union Tribune*. He switched careers and is now an associate professor of English at DePauw University.

Lisa Ampleman is the author of two full-length collections of poetry, *Romances* (LSU Press, forthcoming in 2020) and *Full Cry* (NFSPS Press, 2013), as well as a chapbook, *I've Been Collecting This to Tell You* (Kent State University Press, 2012). Her poems have appeared or are forthcoming in *Poetry, Kenyon Review Online, 32 Poems, Image, Massachusetts Review, New Ohio Review, New South*, Poetry Daily, and Verse Daily. Born and raised in St. Louis, she now lives in Cincinnati, where she is the managing editor of the *Cincinnati Review*.

Alice Azure's most recent poems have appeared in *Yellow Medicine Review*, *Aazhoomom: Convergence, Indigenous Art Exhibition, Thinking Continental: Writing the Planet One Place at a Time*, and the e-magazine, *Dawnland Voices 2.0*. She lives in the St. Louis metropolitan area and is a member of the St. Louis Poetry Center.

María Balogh is a poet, essayist, fiction writer, Caribbean folkloric dancer, and educator, originally from South America, but she is now living in the greater St. Louis area. She has two books published, one in Spanish and one in English, and she teaches Spanish at the University of Missouri-St. Louis.

Sophia Benoit is a writer who spent her first eighteen years in St. Louis before moving away from her family to go live in sunny Los Angeles, a fact that they have still not accepted. She has written for *Allure*, the *Guardian*, the *Cut*, and *Refinery29*, and currently writes for *GQ*. She misses Provel cheese every day.

Rachel Brand is from Kirkwood, Missouri. She graduated from Illinois College with a BA in English, with a concentration in creative writing as well as a minor in gender and women's studies. When not out at The Grove, she can be found taking an excessive amount of pictures of her beagle, Lulu.

Josh Burbridge is an urban historian and writer who has studied St. Louis firsthand working for the St. Louis Public Library and the Landmarks Association of St. Louis. He currently works at the National Archives in North St. Louis County. A native of Elsberry, Missouri, he lives in the Dutchtown neighborhood in South St. Louis.

Kierstan Carter is a first year PhD student in African and African American Studies and Government at Harvard, specializing in twentieth century Black literatures and political theory. She is the creator of convergingcity. com, a co-founder of the Contexture Network, and an avid photographer.

Vincent Casaregola is a professor of English and director of film studies at St. Louis University. He teaches American literature and film, creative writing, rhetorical studies, and composition. He has published poetry in a number of journals, most recently in *The Examined Life, Natural Bridge, WLA, Dappled Things, 2River, Work, Lifelines,* and *Blood and Thunder*. He was awarded the 2017 Best in Poetry Award from *Blood and Thunder*. He works in midtown St. Louis and he lives in South County St. Louis.

Christopher Alex Chablé is a father and poet in St. Louis. A graduate of the University of Missouri, his work has most recently appeared in *Aaduna, 2River View, San Pedro River Review,* and *Sunset Liminal*.

Marie Chewe-Elliott is a writer, poet, and speaker who resides in North St. Louis County.

Katelyn Delvaux works as an English instructor in St. Louis and serves on the poetry staff for *Rivet*. She was the recipient of Wichita State University's Poetry Fellowship (2013), a National Endowment for the Humanities Summer Scholar award (2016), and most recently, she has been a summer scholar at the Poetry Foundation in Chicago (2017).

Lindy Drew studied at the International Center of Photography and then received a Masters of Social Work and Public Health from the Washington University in St. Louis. In 2014, she co-founded and began photographing for Humans of St. Louis (HOSTL), a 501(c)3 nonprofit that shares an intimate look into the lives and struggles of the people of St. Louis, one photo and story at a time. Lindy's work has been published in *St. Louis Magazine*, *St. Louis Post-Dispatch*, *Riverfront Times*, *The Village Voice*, and *Fodor's Travel Guides*. More of her work can be seen at www.lindydrew.com.

Lyndsey Ellis is a fiction writer, essayist, and cultural worker. She was a recipient of the San Francisco Foundation's Joseph Henry Jackson Literary Award in 2016 for her fiction, which explores intergenerational struggle and resiliency in the Midwest. Her writing appears in *Joyland*, *Entropy*, *Jamaica Observer*, *Shondaland*, the *Stockholm Review of Literature*, and elsewhere.

Matthew Freeman is the author of seven collections of poetry, most recently *Trying to Take a Nap,* which was published by Kattywompus Press. He holds an MFA from the University of Missouri and conducts a workshop at the Independence Center.

Eileen G'Sell is a regular contributor to *Salon, VICE,* and the *Boston Review,* among other publications. She currently teaches rhetoric and poetry at Washington University in St. Louis, and creative writing at the Prison Education Project at Missouri Eastern Correctional Center. Her book *Life After Rugby* is now available through Gold Wake Press.

Pamela Garvey is the author of the collection of poetry *Seven Miles Deep* (Five Oaks Press, 2017). Her poetry, prose, and book reviews have appeared in *Esquire, Missouri Review, Margie, Spoon River Poetry Review,* the *North American Review*, and many other journals. She lives in the city of St. Louis with her teenage son, giant dog, and bearded dragon.

Vivian Gibson began writing essays about her childhood in St. Louis after retirement. Her current project is a memoir collection entitled *The Last Children of Mill Creek.*

Debora Grandison is a twenty-nine-year heart disease and diabetes survivor. She serves as a community health advocate and is an inspirational writer, speaker, and poet. She discovered that there's healing in writing!

Galen Gritts is a longtime St. Louis resident who graduated from the University of Missouri-St. Louis in 1975. He is a member of the St. Louis Native Partnerships and Programming Alliance and has been recognized for his work in advocating for Native American representation in business, science, and the arts. He is a member of the Cherokee Nation of Oklahoma.

Layla Azmi Goushey is an associate professor of English at a community college in St. Louis, Missouri. She holds an MFA in Creative Writing and a certificate in the Teaching of Writing from the University of Missouri-St. Louis, where she is also pursuing a PhD in Adult Education: Teaching and Learning Processes. Professor Goushey's scholarly work is focused on Arab and Arab American literature and culture.

Kaitlyn Hough graduated from Lindenwood University in 2016 with a degree in communication. She currently resides in St. Peters, Missouri, and volunteers as the social media coordinator for the literary magazine *River Styx.*

John Hicks is an emerging poet. His poems have been published or accepted for publication by *I-70 Review, First Literary Review-East, Panorama, Midnight Circus, Sky Island Journal,* and others.

Jane Ellen Ibur is the author of *Both Wings Flappin', Still Not Flyin'* and *The Little Mrs./Misses* both published by PenUltimate Press. She has garnered much recognition as an arts educator with over thirty-five years experience teaching writing in public schools, jails, museums, residential schools, and social service agencies, with veterans, homeless men, the young, and old.

Kelly Kiehl Davis is currently a PhD candidate in English at the University of Cincinnati and holds an MFA from Bowling Green State University. Her stories and poems have appeared in or are forthcoming from *Contrary Magazine, Psychopomp Magazine, Passages North,* the *Butter,* and elsewhere.

Asher Kohn is an urban planner and writer from the Midwest who lived in St. Louis from 2009-2013. He has written about and studied urban environments and migrations broadly.

Robert Langellier is a freelance writer based in St. Louis. He's worked variously as a long-haul truck driver, a conservationist, a trails worker, and a magazine journalist.

Caitlin Lee's creative research practice weaves in themes of rust-belt urbanism and collective agency. The writing and the engagement tools she develops employ aspects of design, public policy, investigative reporting, and popular education.

Umar Lee is a freelance writer and activist born and raised in North St. Louis County and he has lived throughout North City, South City, and the west side. Umar has been published previously in the *Nation*, the *Guardian*, *Politico*, the *St. Louis Noir* anthology, and numerous other places.

Mark Loehrer is a graduate student at the University of Missouri-St. Louis studying history. He is interested in public history and the intersection of race and space in city planning. Mark is producer of the *St. Louis Speaks* podcast with host Umar Lee.

Miriam Morris and her parents lived in St. Louis and moved to University City, Missouri. Miriam's quest is to share and preserve the legacy of her father David Friedman. Her search for lost and looted art led to discoveries, exhibitions, and a worldwide revival of an artist obscured by the Nazi regime.

Joan Niesen grew up in West County, hasn't lived in St. Louis since she left for college in 2006, and has never once referred to any other city as "home." These days, she lives in Chicago, is a staff writer at *Sports Illustrated*, and since she knows you're about to ask: she went to Viz.

Devin O'Shea lives in Chicago and is a graduate student in Northwestern's MFA program. His fiction has been featured in *Midwestern Gothic*, he is a reading editor at *TriQuarterly*, and he grew up in Richmond Heights, St. Louis. Devin is writing a novel about the Veiled Prophet Society.

The Rev. Dr. Steven Peebles is a native of Kinloch and is the fourth of five sons of Bennie and Ollie Peebles. Dr. Peebles is a graduate of the Glad Tidings Bible College of St. Louis, where he earned a PhD in systematic theology. Dr. Peebles is married to Pashan Peebles and they have two children, daughter Jasmine and son, Anthony. He is also an auxiliary chaplain of the St. Louis County Police Department.

"**Kirstee Pemberton** is an eleven-year-old fifth grader, born November 24, 1991, who is currently attending Rose Acres Elementary School. She has two sisters, Katelin and Kassidy, and two cats named Annie and Tobie. Kirstee is sweet, caring, and very brave. She loves to play sports, especially softball and swimming. She likes to collect stickers. Kirstee also likes to ride roller coasters." *Kirstee passed away in 2004. She wrote this autobiography for a class assignment.*

Nartana Premachandra is a writer, classical Indian dancer, and president of Dances of India, one of the oldest classical Indian dance companies in the United States. She was born in St. Louis at a time when "Indian" only meant "Cherokee."

Clark Randall is a freelance writer based in St. Louis, Missouri. He studies the historical processes of segregation and suburbanization in the region.

Rebecca Rivas is a staff reporter and video editor for the *St. Louis American*, an African American weekly in St. Louis since 1928. Believing strongly in the power of community journalism, she has worked in community news, largely Hispanic and African American publications, since 2000.

Veneta Rizvic is a reporter and social media manager at the *St. Louis Business Journal*, where she's worked since March 2015. Veneta previously worked as a journalist in Cedar Rapids, Iowa. She attended the University of Missouri in Columbia and currently resides in St. Louis County with her husband and cat.

Nick Sacco is a historian and writer. He holds a master's degree in history from IUPUI and two bachelor's degrees from Lindenwood University. A St. Louis native, Nick has lived in the metro area for most of his life. In his free time he enjoys playing upright and electric bass, spending time with his fiancée, and finding the next great restaurant to visit in the St. Louis area.

Maja Sadikovic received her MFA from the University of Missouri-St. Louis. She has been writing since her childhood and is interested in topics of identity crisis within the former Yugoslav people. She speaks four languages and hopes to pursue a PhD in comparative literature.

Ron Scott is a retired psychologist living in Kirkwood, Missouri. He is married to Marilyn Scott, and together they have a blended family of five children and eight grandchildren. He has worked as a welfare case manager and a parole agent in Los Angeles, as a university teacher in Richmond, Virginia, and at the University of Missouri-St. Louis, and as a psychotherapist in St. Louis County.

Inda Schaenen is a writer and teacher in the Normandy Schools Collaborative. Her most recent book *is Speaking of Fourth Grade: What Listening to Kids Tells Us About School in America* (The New Press, 2015).

Dick Shimamoto was born in Lodi, California, three weeks before the Japanese attack on Pearl Harbor. Brothers Dave and Ed were born in a Japanese American relocation camp in Rohwer, Arkansas. They grew up in South St. Louis and each graduated from the University of Missouri-Rolla. They have been active as volunteers in the Japanese American Citizen's League (JACL) and numerous other organizations over the years.

Adam Steevens is the author of *The United States of Repression*. He is a St. Louis native who lives in the Shaw neighborhood. When Adam isn't writing, he enjoys watching ice hockey and drinking bourbon.

Megan Stringer is graduating from DePaul University in Chicago in autumn 2018 with a major in journalism and a minor in creative writing. Her poetry has appeared in *Crook & Folly*, DePaul's arts and literary magazine, and was chosen by Kevin Coval as the second best piece of poetry in Edition 38.

Ibro Suljic is an entrepreneur and immigrant who came to the United States in 1996 as a refugee from Bosnia. He moved to St. Louis in 2007.

Aisha Sultan is a syndicated columnist, filmmaker, and speaker. Her work has run in more than a hundred publications, including the *Atlantic*, the *Wall Street Journal*, and the *Washington Post*. She has won several national awards recognizing her writing, including the Knight Wallace Fellowship at the University of Michigan. Her work explores social change and how it impacts families. She lives with her husband and two children in St. Louis.

Deborah Jackson Taffa earned her MFA at the University of Iowa in 2013. In 2018, she co-wrote a documentary, *The Trail of Tears,* for PBS, won the Ellen Meloy Desert Writer's Award, and was named A Public Space fellow by the Brooklyn magazine. Her writing has appeared or is forthcoming in *A Public Space, Salon*, the *Rumpus, The Best American Travel Writing,* and other places. You can find more about her at https://deborahtaffa.com

jason vasser-elong is a poet and essayist that was born and raised in St. Louis, Missouri, but has maternal ancestral roots in Cameroon, Central Africa. In 2014 the Cameroon Royal Council gave the name Elong (Eh-long) to him, and after embracing it, he added that name to reflect his family's legacy. He earned an MFA in creative writing from the University of Missouri-St. Louis after studying cultural anthropology and presenting his ethnographic research *Rhyme and Reason: Poetics as Societal Dialogue.*

Eamonn Wall is the author of *Junction City: New and Selected Poems 1990-2015* (Salmon Poetry, Ireland, 2015), among other poetry publications. Prose books include *Writing the Irish West: Ecologies and Traditions* (Notre Dame, 2011) and *From the Sin-é Café to the Black Hills: Notes on the New Irish* (Wisconsin, 2000). A native of Ireland, Eamonn Wall lives in Webster Groves and works at the University of Missouri-St. Louis where he is the Smurfit-Stone Corporation Professor of Irish Studies/International Studies and Programs.

Robin Wheeler is a writer, chef, mother, and a St. Louis transplant from the western wilds of Missouri. She's lived in Belleville, Illinois, since 2007. Her book *Woody Guthrie's True Love* is forthcoming.